FIFTY BALES OF HAY

Roger Evans

Britain's Favourite Dairy Farmer

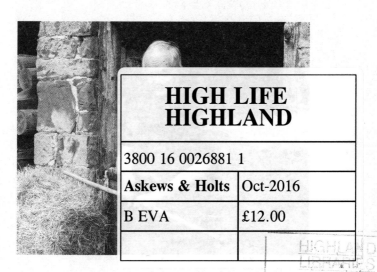

MERLIN UNWIN BOOKS

First published in Great Britain by Merlin Unwin Books, 2016

Merlin Unwin Books Ltd
Palmers House, 7 Corve Street
Ludlow, Shropshire SY8 1DB
U.K.
www.merlinunwin.co.uk

The author asserts his moral right to be identified with this work.

Designed and set in Bembo 11pt by Merlin Unwin
Printed and bound by CPI Group (UK) Ltd, Croydon, CR0 4YY

ISBN 978-1-910723-30-2

To my grandchildren
Rhys, Tomos, Katie,
David and Hannah

23 MARCH 2014

A few weeks ago I was looking for harbingers of spring. I'm still looking. It's not that cold but nothing seems to be happening. The grass fields and the winter corn are not moving. It's true that nowhere around here has anyone put any fertiliser on yet, it's too wet, but the beginning of March, surely something should be on the move. But it's not, I'm sure that it's because the ground is saturated and cold. There are no daffodils out around here yet. I've scanned the hedgerows in known sheltered places and there's not a green leaf to be seen. Then yesterday, a Sunday afternoon, all that changed, spring is on its way. I heard my first pack of motorbikes tearing their way through the countryside.

★★★

There was a time when if you saw a fox about in the daytime, it was such a noteworthy event that you would introduce the fact into your conversation. 'Saw a fox this morning.' 'Where was that?' It's not that big a deal any more. Mert my dog has never been shut up at night since I've had him and you can hear him barking about the yard every night, I assume at foxes. I can't think of anything else that would make him bark, he doesn't bark at all in the daytime. In fact he's mostly asleep in the daytime, probably tired out from barking at foxes all night! But we do see foxes about the yard in the daytime and we know that they are about at night, because David has cows calving at the moment and he goes around these cows late at night, and he sees foxes all the time. So it seems reasonable to conclude that that is what Mert is barking at.

The daytime foxes take more understanding. They will stroll by at about 30 yards distance, seemingly unconcerned about the human activity all around them. They don't look that fit, they look mangy and diseased, and that is, I suppose, what draws them to our yard. They are probably struggling to survive out in the wild and are drawn to our yard where they probably eat calf food and the like from out of food troughs. They may well be urban foxes that haven't adjusted to the challenges of living in the wild, and maybe never will.

29 MARCH 2014

My eldest granddaughter is 13. At school, in an English lesson, they are discussing writing. She tells the teacher 'My Pop is a writer.' (They all call me Pop, at least the grandchildren do.) The teacher is really interested in this information so Katie tells her that I write articles for magazines and newspapers and that three books have been published. 'I wonder if your Pop would come to talk to us about writing?' 'Yes he would,' says Katie. 'Perhaps you'll ask him.' 'No need to, he'll come.' 'Yes, but you have to ask him first.' 'No need to, he'll come.' 'How can you be so sure he will come?' ''Cus he loves me.' Quite made my day.

★★★

I've got this friend, he's a Scot, but he can't help that. He goes on endlessly about Scottish rugby every season and the 'new dawn' due to arrive every year. He tells me that he has this ambition to go to see Scotland play Wales at the Millennium stadium but he can never get a ticket. I didn't get where I am today without being able to put my hand on tickets for Wales' matches but I kept this quiet. We have an established carload that go to all Wales matches in Cardiff and always go to one away game as well. But friends had weddings and holidays and I had room in the car so I told him a couple of months ago that I would take him to the Scotland game. Fortuitously as it turns out. So he's getting very excited and goes on endlessly about it and after we lose to England at Twickenham he senses victory. Because he's on such a high I tell him that there are conditions to coming with me. 'What conditions?' 'No kilts, no guitar (he's always playing his guitar), and no Saltire draped in the back window of the car.' I've seen sad faces in my time but rarely one as sad as his, which told me that a kilt and a flag were definitely part of his plan. I was actually very surprised that when I picked him up, neither were evident. Despite my warning I expected him to do his own thing, and I wouldn't really have been worried if he had, but he wasn't taking a chance on being left behind. As it turned out Wales won 51-3 which kept him quiet on the way home and will probably keep him quiet about Scot's rugby for 12 months. By which time they will have had the vote on Scottish independence and if it's a 'Yes' vote we will send him back anyway.

***

The reign of terror inflicted on our local community by our turkeys continues undiminished. One near neighbour couldn't get her children out of the house to take them to school and they appeared on her Facebook page, as 'killer turkeys'. I've easily sorted that; I just let them out later in the morning. It's all very funny, for spectators, but it's getting very close to being a real issue and I might have to take measures of containment. At present they behave like dogs that might bite you, except that people are mostly wary of a strange dog whereas they approach the turkeys (well they do the first time anyway), completely unsuspecting of what lies in wait.

I don't like being harassed by dogs. I've got a friend whose dogs are notorious, and I will not get out of the truck on his yard until I'm sure that there are no dogs loose, or if there are, that he's about as well, to control them. There's the story of an agricultural salesman who was terrified of farm dogs. The dogs for their part would sense this and give him a hard time. One farm he went to had a really nasty dog that lived in a kennel on a chain whenever it wasn't working with sheep or cattle. To get to the farmhouse there was about a metre of safety between the length of the chain and an adjoining building. The salesman would apparently spreadeagle himself, back against the wall, and inch himself past the snapping dog. One day, business done, he came out of the house, ready to repeat the ordeal, to be confronted by an empty chain. I'm not sure if a chain can be empty but, whatever, it was dog-less. This wasn't, from his point of view, a good thing. At least when the dog was on the chain he knew where it was. Now he didn't. And if he didn't know where it was, where was it? So he made his way back to his car with even more caution, his back still against the wall, thus reducing the possible area of attack. Inch by precarious inch he got back to his car, making the last yard or two in a panic-driven run. Into the car, slam the door and safe. Except that he was not safe. Sitting on the passenger seat, hackles up, teeth bared, was the dog. The lads who worked on the farm had put it in his car whilst he was in the farmhouse!

5 April 2014

It's Saturday night in the pub. The participants split into two different groups. In one group are the tractor drivers and farmers. Their conversation is quite animated: it's all about tractors and implements and what they've been doing with them since they last met. I swear they use more red diesel in the pub on Saturday nights than they do all week. I don't mean to mock them because they spend very long hours alone in a tractor cab at this time of year with just the radio for company, so what they are doing now is a sort of release for all the thoughts that have accumulated during the week.

One of them is telling the rest how his boss has turned the sprayer over and this is the dominant theme. They all have similar stories to tell and also of near misses. Their biggest problem is getting their own story in, and as far as I can tell there's always two or three talking at the same time. The tractor drivers and farmers are all standing at the bar; the other group, their wives, girlfriends and partners, are all sitting around a table. That's where I am. You wouldn't believe what you can find out sitting down quietly with a group of women. Much of it is not for the faint-hearted. To start with they all have their phones out and are comparing stuff that's on Facebook. There's a bit of a local spat going on and I can't believe what some people will write down for the rest of the world to read. I have a maxim in life that if you have something really blunt to say to someone, who has perhaps messed you about, it's far better to tell them than writing it down. If they don't like what you have said, which is after all, the main purpose of what you have to say, if it's in writing they can keep it, put it away somewhere and get it out to look at again and again and thus nurture the disagreement for years and years to come. If some plain-speaking is needed, and it sometimes is, best to say it and move on. Can't see that happening with some of the stuff I'm reading on Facebook, they might not keep it for years but they know that it has gone out to a very wide audience which all serves to compound the issue. But we move on.

Another lady turns up. They've all been to one of those sales parties and she's brought what they've ordered. Of course they all have to open every jar and tube to revisit what they've bought. There's beauty potions, oil and ointments everywhere and they are all trying them out. I get to try them out as well. Soon I've had a little bit of this and a little bit of that rubbed into the back of my hand and a squirt of different deodorants applied in different places 'Try this one, Rog.'

★★★

On Sunday night at the pub it's all men, mostly the same men. So they start picking on me. 'Used to be a hard rugby player and now he's gone all girly. Sitting with the women all night and talking about creams and make-up.' I let them get on with it; let them have their amusement. It will soon be my turn. My turn, when it comes, is an opportunity to ask questions. 'Which of us, spent last night in the pub talking about tractors and farming? And which of us was sitting with a group of women, who took turns to hold his hand and rub various lotions into it?' They all reflect on this. There's no more talk of me being 'girly'. In fact I'm fairly sure I've won the day.

Just had to take the man to read the meter which is deep in turkey territory. He tells me that dogs are the most scary part of his job; well they were until now anyway. He says he's never been chased by a turkey before, he says he can't wait to tell his mates. I notice that he kept very close to me when I took him up the garden.

13 APRIL 2014

I had to fly to Glasgow yesterday for an overnight stay. It's a journey I used to do most weeks at one time in my life so it was a bit of a trip down memory lane. How things have changed! I'm heading for the check-in desk and am stopped in my tracks by a young man who shows me that if I put my passport into this machine, a ticket comes out, push another button and the ticket comes out for the next day. I didn't have to check a bag in because I'd got what I needed in my laptop bag. Toothbrush, electric shaver, clean shirt and spare pair of knickers in case I had an accident. I'm a slightly reluctant user of this new technology. For years I steadfastly refused to use a cashpoint. I used to go into the bank and cash a cheque. The girls behind the counter used to say every time 'You don't need to come in here for cash, you can get it out of the machine.' And every time I would point out that if we all did that there would be no need for pretty girls sitting at bank counters. And they would smile at me indulgently. Now the bank is a clothes shop. Airports are good for people watching. I always notice that people will push and jostle to get onto the plane. And when you arrive at your destination, they push and jostle to get off.

★★★

At long last I set off with the roller. I've been looking forward to this for some time, which some people might think a bit sad but I think that I am lucky to enjoy the job I have. If you enjoy your work, then it isn't really work at all, is it? I'm off to roll two fields we rent a couple of miles away. Getting out with the roller is my chance to scrutinise, close up, all of my fields and the flora and fauna within them. Which is, in itself, a problem with these two particular fields. They are close to a busy road and a busy village so there's no fauna about, and the flora is a bit of a problem. The two fields used to be part of a larger farm which, at one time, grew daffodils commercially.

One of the fields, the closest one to the buildings, has a huge number of daffodils growing in it; they are a picture in the spring sunshine. As you possibly also know, daffodils are my favourite flower, because they herald the arrival of spring and because they are a Welsh symbol. It grieves me to do it but I'm just about to roll them flat. There's too many to dodge around them so a good rolling is what they get, though I do get off the tractor and pick a goodly bunch to take home for the missus. (Which completely throws her; in fact it makes her suspicious.)

When I've finished, there are nice dark and light green stripes up and down the fields, just how I like it. It's a contentious issue on this farm, rolling. We've got a consultant who is driven by cutting costs. Which is OK up to a point. But he is given to walking about the yard and kicking things like the roller, and saying 'you need to sell that.' I tell him I don't. He asks what I need it for and I say rolling, and he says land rarely needs rolling and I say I like the land to be rolled and he says it's a cost in fuel and wages and I say but I don't get any wages. And so it goes on. But the roller is still here and I continue to use it. And in due course I will have all my silage fields looking lovely with stripes everywhere and also in due course I will meet one or both of my landlords and I know, from previous experiences, that they will say 'you've got the farm looking well this spring' and I will say to them 'thank you', and I will say to the consultant 'How do you put a value on that?'

★★★

Every spring the story of aggressive cock pheasants makes it into the national dailies and sometimes even on television. This always surprises me because it is such a common phenomenon in pheasant country. I've always assumed that these stories only make it to the top of the pile on slow news days and I'm probably right. I've reported on it often enough. Yesterday I got into the truck out on the yard and before I could start up, the mobile phone rang. So I'm sitting there in the truck answering the phone and this cock pheasant starts to cross the yard about 20 yards in front of me. There's a real sense of purpose to its progress, it's low to the ground, but it's obviously on some sort of mission, there's stealth there and menace. I can tell by its demeanour that it's protecting its territory but as yet I can't see from what. Also about 20 yards in front of me is the shed where we calve our cows and one of the cows has her head through the feed barrier and is eating some silage.

The pheasant takes the last ten yards at a sprint, races up to the cow and gives it a sharp peck on the nose. The startled cow jerks back out of sight. Satisfied with itself, the pheasant stand up on tiptoe and flaps its wings in triumph. But only for fractions of a second. It goes back down into its stealth position and positively sprints back the way it had come. So, I wonder, what's going on here? I soon find out. Out of a bunch of nettles at the top of the yard bursts a much bigger cock pheasant. He races down the yard in pursuit, not in a direct line but in a diagonal run that will cut the first pheasant off from wherever he is heading. It's several minutes before the dominant cock returns. That will teach a pheasant not to peck my cows.

19 APRIL 2014

Here are the headlines today: 'Saturated fat isn't bad for your heart.' So what does that mean? Well saturated fats turn up naturally in dairy products, products like milk and butter. Before we go further, let's remind ourselves that milk is nature's most complete, natural food, and by some distance. And as we go further let's just remind ourselves that for over 40 years the saturated fats in dairy products have been blamed for heart disease and, to a lesser extent, obesity. I used to be on something called the Dairy Council, which for years has been saying that the saturated fats in dairy products have been unfairly stigmatised and maligned by researchers whose research was funded by the industries that produce the spreads and oils that compete with natural dairy products. Here's another quote from the article: 'It is time to bust the myth of the role of saturated fat in heart disease, which was based on faulty interpretation of scientific studies.' It's possible that not many of you are still reading this, perhaps you've switched off and moved on, but this myth not only affected dairy farmers' lives, it's affected yours as well. For dairy farmers it has devalued what they produce by saying dairy products undermine health, and not saying it occasionally but on and on for 40 years. For you consumers it's affected your lives, because when you walk past the milk section of your supermarket, there's actually been no need for all those endless rows of skimmed and semi-skimmed and 1% fat milks, no need for low fat cheeses, no need for low fat dairy products of any sort.

The real culprits in dietary well-being seem to be sugar, salt and processed foods. And isn't it just possible that if we all had cereal with proper milk on it for breakfast and toast with butter on, we wouldn't be hungry again by 11 o'clock, and fill up on processed foods that are not so good for us? What beggars belief is that if saturated fat being responsible for heart disease is a myth, where were all the scientists at places like the Food Standards Agency who allowed all this misinformation to go out? And how can people vilify an industry for so long and get away with it? My breakfast most days is two pieces of toast and marmite, but I do trawl the fridge for scraps to eat, left by grazing grandchildren and for anything that's past its sell-by-date. One of my favourites is fried tomatoes and I find some that are getting a bit soft. I cut them up and put them in the frying pan. I pick up the big bottle of sunflower oil that always stands next to the cooker. And I put it down again.

I go back to the fridge and find some butter, cut off a lump and smack it in the frying pan. So there! And it tastes so much better. Milk that has the fat in it, and full fat is only 4%, by the way, tastes better. Try it.

★★★

I've just been rolling our largest field, 42 acres, which is a slow long job. I suppose I was born of an age when we had to do mental arithmetic. My grandchildren are amazed sometimes at what I can work out. They reach for the calculators on their phones – a few years ago it would have been calculators – we didn't have any of that. The nearest we had to that would have been a slide rule, I could see how they worked but never owned one, only smart arses owned one. But I can often work something out in my head quicker than they can fire up their calculators. I also have a sort of shorthand way of doing it. If I wanted to multiply 17 x 19 for example, I would multiply 17 by 20 and then knock off 17, easy peasy. Anyway I'm back on the roller, slowly going up and down the field and I work out, all in my head, how many square yards there are in the field and from there how many square feet so I divide the square feet by the width of the roller which is 10ft and convert back the feet to miles with the result that to roll this field I cover 34 miles. Plus the distance I travel at the ends of the fields where I turn around to go back down again, which distance is not inconsiderable. I'm travelling at about ten kilometres an hour. I expect you are amazed at how effortlessly I have switched from imperial measure to metric but the tractor is French and I can read the speed on the dashboard. So that's around six miles an hour which if you are on overtime rates is too quick but if you don't get paid, like me, is not quick enough.

But we mustn't forget the wildlife, and today the wildlife is very quiet. I've not seen a hare all day but apart from pheasants the most numerous bird is the skylark. I reckon there's twice as many as when I rolled the same field last year. I don't pretend to claim any credit for that. But then again, it's obvious that I'm not doing anything that is detrimental to nature. I take pleasure from that. And pride.

26 April 2014

I've been to Northern Ireland for 24 hours this week, to a dinner. It's such a nice place and such nice people. Some of the people actually do say things like Jim McDonald used to say on *Coronation Street*, which always seemed to be a bit over the top. Things like, 'You need to get a taxi to go to the airport at nine o'clock, so you do.' It's quite a strange phenomenon when complete strangers come up to you, introduce themselves, and then ask of you, 'How's Mert?' He, Mert the dog, is completely unaware of how famous he is. So how is he? Well he's getting on a bit now and he's put on a bit of weight since I had him castrated, something I will always regret. But then he doesn't roam the roads any more on romantic walkabouts, so it might have saved his life. I don't take him for long days on the tractor any more because I can see that after a couple of hours, he's not that comfortable, but I do take him if it's a short outing. When I don't take him he stands on the yard watching me go and gives me a look that breaks my heart, and if he was a dog in a cartoon, there would be a bubble coming out from his mouth that said, 'Bastard.'

He never ceases to amaze me with how he reacts to what I say to him. We were going around the cattle the other day and came across a husband and wife out jogging. They were all expensive matching jogging outfits and not much jog. I'm sure you get the picture. I'm not sure where they lived but you could easily tell that it was no longer such a good an idea as they thought it was when they had set out. In fact it was clearly more of a walk than a jog, it was only a jog when someone like me came along who was watching. I slowed down to pass them in the narrow lane. Mert wasn't even looking out of the window, he was curled up in the back of the truck. I just said quietly, half to myself in fact, 'Just look at the state of these two.' Mert leaped to his feet, put his head out of the window, and frightened the life out of them, in fact, because the lane was narrow I don't think he was far off biting them, which is what joggers are for. They tried to jog on, nonchalantly, but I could see in the mirror that they only jogged for about 50 yards and then they were walking again.

When I say we are out in the truck, I actually mean an old four-wheel drive vehicle. Most of my neighbours spend thousands of pounds on quad bikes and mules, we buy old 4x4s, we're into collecting old Shoguns at the moment, a really battered one to fetch the cows and carry the electric fencing paraphernalia and a less battered one to use on the roads. So Mert travels in the bit at the very back.

Now here's a strange thing. Most of our journeys are on minor roads and tracks and fields but when we are returning home, the last half a mile of our journey is on a B-road that runs past the farm. As soon as we get to the junction where we join the B-road, Mert always clambers over the seats and stands with his head on my shoulder. In fact, it's not so much his head, it's his neck and his head is pressed down onto my chest, so I can easily stroke him. It's not done occasionally or anywhere else, just when we go through that junction. For many years I had a role in the dairy industry that would take me away from the farm every week. Sometimes for a couple of days, sometimes for the whole week. I can never remember a single occasion when I didn't arrive home, open the car door and his head would come through the gap onto my knee. He still does that whenever I come home now, if I've been away for ten minutes or a couple of days. Animals can give us a clear lead when it comes to loyalty and devotion.

★★★

Just as an aside. It's 9pm and I'm thinking of bed and book, and my wife says 'You'd better get your evening suit out and see what state you left it in.' This is the evening before I go to Belfast to a black tie dinner. I don't wear this sort of outfit very often, not sure why but I don't enjoy wearing one. It sounds a bit unkind, asking what state I left it in, but there is a reality to it. After a night out, it is always possible that there is food left on your suit but it is always a possibility that on arriving home from a late night out, there are calving cows to visit and for the tired dairy farmer, to go upstairs and get changed is quite a big job: far easier to slip your wellies on and go out in your suit. It is the mission of all cows to try to cover everything with what they excrete at their rear end and some of this ends up on your suit. Anyway, to return to our story, by 9.15pm I cannot find the dress suit so my wife has to come and have a look. She's not best pleased because she's watching a series on TV. I could pause it for her but by this time, sharp words have been exchanged, so serve her right.

By 10.15pm, by which time we have scoured every wardrobe, cupboard and every coat hook in the house, we come to the conclusion that I no longer have a dress suit. Those of you who are married will understand that by this time some quite animated conversations have taken place. Most of the conversations centre on my opinion that it is a wifely duty to care for and clean her husband's clothes. I lose this argument but deep down I know that my mother would have done it. Exhausted by our search, we decide that I have either left it somewhere or someone has borrowed it and we can't remember who. I try to press the latter scenario, mainly because I suspect it's the former. So I have to go out in a rush the next day and buy a new one. I'm not best pleased, my inclination would be to scour the charity shops for one, but there's no time for that. The man in the shop thinks it's hilarious and my reply, when he suggests I go the whole way and buy a new shirt as well, is unprintable.

3 MAY 2014

I had a reader from Wiltshire contact me to commend me on the piece I wrote about the pundits finally admitting that the fat content in milk is actually a health benefit. He went on to say that I had missed out an important part of the message. And my omission was an important one. Osteoporosis is a serious condition of the weakening of the bones. Surveys predict that in an ageing population it will be of epidemic proportions. Now I'm no scientist but it seems common sense to me that when you remove the fat content, you take with it a lot of the important mineral content as well. And within that mineral content is a lot of the calcium you need for stronger bones. So we are about to see the first generation reaching retirement age that have possibly spent a goodly percentage of their lives drinking skimmed milk. There is no upside to all that unless perhaps that the first people to fall down and break some bones, are the ones who have advocated removing all the fat for the last 40 years. Shame that.

★★★

It's Sunday morning and we, Mert and I, are off around the dry cows and in-calf heifers which are on their last week on the kale and turnips. There's about 50 of them in this group. I should know how many, but there's cows going home to calve most days and newly dry cows joining every week so the numbers are constantly changing. It doesn't matter really how many there are because they are almost impossible to count. The dry cows ignore me and continue what they are doing, be it grazing or lying down. The in-calf heifers are a different matter, they are well full of themselves and swarm around the truck looking for mischief. A chew of a wing mirror here, a chew of the wiper on the back door, a good rub on the headlights, it's all good fun.

Mert is busy in the back biting, the glass and barking at them. I can count the dry cows but the heifers don't keep still long enough. So my husbandry duties involve a good look around all corners of the field and a good look at all the stock, to see if anything is amiss. A blob of white under a hedge catches my eye and I drive across to it. As I get nearer I can see it is a calf. (Some dry cows don't make it home before they calve!) The calf has tucked itself into some briars as a sort of hiding place. These calves will secrete themselves away when born outside, in long grass or nettles, as an instinctive ploy to keep them away from predators. It's the bovine equivalent of keeping your head down. I pull up alongside the calf. It doesn't move but I can see it is fine. It's tight against the fence and on the fence is a raven. Like the calf, the raven doesn't move. If my arm was a foot longer I could almost touch it. The raven has spotted the calf and it is obvious it thinks it will claim it as a prize. It dwells there for quite a time, as if challenging me. Eventually it flaps lazily away and I get out and rouse the calf and push it back towards its mother. A raven can't kill a big calf but I've probably saved its eyes.

★★★

I'm a great reader. I was brought up to respect books. I never throw a book away. There's two stacks of books in my bedroom that would comfortably make a cubic metre if you were to put them on a pallet. I don't throw them away in case I want to revisit them. And the books I revisit the most often are the works of Dylan Thomas. Now I would be the first to say that I find some of his poetry difficult. I came to the conclusion some time ago that when he wrote some of it he was either drunk or mad, or possibly both and you yourself would probably understand it better if you were drunk or mad as well. Then there's *Under Milk Wood*. I've read it so many times. It's the centenary of Dylan Thomas and there's a production of *Under Milk Wood* on tour at present.

We went to see it last week. We took my eldest granddaughter and she loved it. He describes things using words that you would never dream of using, yet having read them they seem so apt and appropriate I'd love to be able to write just a few lines like he has. I've tried a few times: 'The cock pheasant, rampant red of comb, struts lordily amongst his hens, he stands on tiptoe, golden plumed and barrel chested and waves his defiance to the world.' 'The moo-licked calf, fat and sleek, nestles warm and safe into the deep grass, turns its lidded face to the warm caress of the sun and dreams of frothy milk around its muzzle and the creamy life that is to come.' Nah, can't do it.

Just as an aside, the same granddaughter who was moved by *Under Milk Wood* has told me that when she leaves school she wants to be a slaughterman in an abattoir. Well someone has to do it.

10 MAY 2014

I'm driving up the track at our other buildings and two walkers appear in front of me having just negotiated the stile out of the fields. They have two dogs with them, a spaniel and a collie. Seeing me approach on the tractor, they put them back on their leads. The dogs are panting excessively, mud up their sides, exhausted. By the look of the couple who own them they, the dogs, didn't get into that state on their leads, because the couple don't look as if they have broken sweat for years. They've been through over a mile on 'my' fields, so what have they chasing? For certain they have been chasing hares, terrorising leverets and eating skylarks' young and eggs. They've probably done more damage to wildlife in half an hour than I could do in a year. I don't say anything, I'm so angry, and you never know where anger will lead. There's been three lapwings up there for two days: wonder if they are still there.

★★★

There's been a lot of wildlife about in the night. When our last lot of point-of-lay pullets went off, some of them staged a breakout and eluded the catching gang. This was a heroic tale, a bit like *The Great Escape*. Over the next few days we managed to gather them up and erected a temporary house for them, the poultry sheds not being available because of cleaning them out for the next lot. It may have been a temporary house but they'd been there a week and none had escaped. Last night Mr Fox paid them a visit, or was it Mrs Fox and all the little foxes? Whatever, there were feathers all over the yard, several missing and 20 dead in their pen.

As if that wasn't bad enough, our cows are grazed on a very disciplined paddock system that is managed by electric fences. It sounds a bit draconian but it isn't, it's all designed to give them as much grass as they can possibly eat every day, with the advantage that the grass is at the very best of nutritional value. A herd of deer has been through in the night and now there's electric fence wire everywhere. What a shambles.

★★★

I wasn't born into a farming family and my first venture into farming on my own account was to buy 12 white day-old chicks that would become layers for me to sell the eggs. I kept them in a shed and run that I built at the bottom of our garden. I was about 12 at the time, so it was not recent, but it was at a time when hybrid strains of poultry were beginning to emerge. The traditional breeds had names like Rhode Island Red and Brown Leghorn and Light Sussex, the new hybrids I remember were called romantic names like 101, which was a very flighty white bird that laid white eggs and 404s which were a more middle-of-the-road bird, a brown bird that laid brown eggs. None of these should be confused with 303s which were army rifles. My little white chicks were Light Sussex crossed with Brown Leghorns which was a very popular cross for laying birds.

Looking back, the only negative to this cross was that they would go broody in the spring and peck lumps out of your hands when you collected the eggs. It was what they called a sex link cross in that the colour of the cockerel, the white Light Sussex, turned up in his female offspring which were all white. Most commercial poultry today are hybrids but genetics are genetics and the sex link still exists. That's why the pullets we rear these days are brown but if we are to find replacements for the departed cockerel Neville, it will be a white cockerel that has slipped through the system. It was not until our last crop of pullets were due to go that we did indeed spot a white cockerel. This may seem strange but in a shed that contains say 20,000 birds, it is not easy to identify individual birds and establish a relationship with them. Once, when we produced broilers, which were white, and 28,000 of them in each shed, I discovered a black chick amongst them. I used to make a point of finding it every day and picking it up and stroking it. One day the chick was in my hands and I was making a fuss of it when I looked down at the floor and there was another black chick looking up at me as if to say, 'Why are you ignoring me today?' So you never know where you are with a lot of poultry. The black chicks didn't make it to anybody's table because the white ones gang up on them and kill them. No comment. So to go back to this cockerel, we've removed him from the sheds and put him with a couple of pullets for company, into the turkey garden so that he can develop into another Neville and eventually terrorise the yard. I've got my doubts about him, thus far there's no aggression. In fact, truth be told, I'm not sure if he knows if he's a Neville or a Nora.

17 MAY 2014

We've just emptied our chicken sheds and the point-of-lay pullets that they contained have gone onto pastures new. Which statement is literally quite true as they have moved on to free range layer units and will soon be laying lots of nice brown eggs. They were all brown pullets but within that there were different strains. I don't think they were different breeds because I am assuming they were all hybrids of some sort. What I do know is that some of them were called Columbian Black Tails, which name has a sort of mystery about it. The main purpose of this story is to tell you that when the poultry go out of the sheds, all the manure has to go out as well. It comes out as a very dusty product (providing there hasn't been a burst with the drinking system!) and it is just a wonderful manure to put back on the land. The balance of it is roughly two parts nitrogen to one each of phosphate and potash. We take the poultry manure around the farm so that all fields get some in turn. Most of the land we rent used to lie in continuous cereal crops which did not benefit from any animal by-products at all.

Ten years on, my neighbours tell me how much the land has improved with the influence of poultry manure, manure from the cattle and the presence of the cattle themselves. We use a lot less artificial fertiliser than we did ten years ago because we've increased the organic matter in the soil, we've put some 'heart' into it. Poultry manure contains some calcium because the birds have to have grit in their diet as part of their digestion and this all helps with the pH of the soil. This organic matter increases the worm population, so it's all win-win. In fact it's win-win as far as the eye can see.

What's poultry manure got to do with hares? Well I've been carting manure for about two days and at one place I travel past on the track to where we tip it is a low bank out of the adjoining field. It's only a couple of feet high, this bank, but at some time a cow has come down it and her rear hoof had slipped and made a gouge-mark in the turf. It's not a cowslip, which is a wild flower, and it's not a skid mark, which can mean something entirely different, it's just a shallow mark in the turf. But tucked into this depression is a hare. She lies there, ears flattened to her body and she's there every time I pass over those two days, carting manure. The tractor wheels pass within a foot of her nose each time I pass but she doesn't move a muscle. On the third day, I go up the same track to see the cattle and she's not there, but there is a tiny leveret there, pressing itself down into the depression very much as its mother has done. Next day there's no sign of either of them, I just hope that they have moved into the cover of the adjoining winter barley field.

★★★

I'm off with the topper to chop off what is left of the kale stalks. The cattle are running on the whole piece now and there's about five or six acres that they went on last, which is about 3ft high with thick hard stalks. The cattle have eaten all the leaves off and they would eat the stalks as well but the kale has had its time, it's time to move onto the next crop. So I'm chopping off the stalks so they will plough in better. At first sight it's just a mess of green tough stalks, but as I move into it with the tractor I find it's full of cock pheasants. It's a sort of sanctuary for bachelor cock pheasants, those that haven't been able to establish a territory around the hedgerow and attract some hens. The cocks are distributed evenly throughout the cover that the kale stalks afford them, and they have a disconsolate air about them. There's surely 50 of them and they are here as losers, losers of fights. They've had enough of fighting which is why they are all spread out.

But life is never as good as it seems. I was telling my 7-year-old grandson this yesterday. I told him 'It's a hard life out there, Dave, you and I had better stick together.' And I had his wide-eyed agreement. So for your cock pheasant nursing his pride and possibly a few wounds, here comes a noisy farmer on a noisy tractor and over the next hour or so he removes this sanctuary you have found and now the next cock pheasant can see you, and the next pheasant to that, and before you know where you are, there are about five groups of ten pheasants in each group, all fighting like hell. And it gets worse, because the dominant cocks around the hedgerows can now see all those possible interlopers, and they charge up the field to the battle as well. Before you know it there are pheasants and feathers flying everywhere. After a quarter of an hour peace is restored, some pheasants have disappeared to continue their nomadic life in the winter wheat in the next field, some have flown as far as the woods. I make my way home on the tractor feeling a bit guilty. I only came up here to tidy the field so I could plough it.

24 MAY 2014

Although the cows have been grazing for some time now, grass growth is still not sufficient for their needs and they are on a half silage, half grass diet at present. All the silage has been eaten at home here now and we have to fetch a load every day from the clamp at the other buildings. It's my job to fetch a fresh load, Saturday and Sunday afternoons, ready for the next day. So there I was yesterday afternoon, tractor and trailer backed into the silage clamp, and I'm on the loader cutting blocks of silage and tipping them into the trailer, except that I'm not really, I'm day dreaming as usual and my mind is miles away. Suddenly there's a loud bang against the window of the cab and from the corner of my eye I see something falling down to the floor. I stop immediately and my first understandable reaction is 'What the hell was that?' My first conclusion is that someone has thrown something and I look carefully around. Nothing. So I look to see what had caught my eye falling to the ground. Down by the front tyre, in full attack mode, actually pecking at the tyre, is a cock pheasant. This clamp is built into the bank and the sides are about 12ft higher than where I am working. The pheasant obviously has his territory in the adjoining hedgerow and has launched himself off to attack me sitting on the loader. Luckily for me he didn't attack the other side of the loader, I've got the door fastened open on that side. Life can be scary working on a farm.

***

I've got a farm secretary. She comes once a fortnight. Whisper it softly but I'm scared of her. I spend a good proportion of my life looking for pieces of paper and she comes and puts some order to it all. I like her a lot but I'm still scared of her. She's got a couple of horses and three Hereford cows that rear their own calves. In the space of one week, two of her cows had twins. She has a problem with one cow, it won't let its calves suckle, so she asks my advice. My advice is that she comes to the pub on a Thursday night and puts the question to the farmers. She passes on that, so I put the question on her behalf. The table is surrounded by instant experts on the subject. 'Tie her back legs together so she can't kick' (sounds like good way of getting kicked yourself), 'Put a cargo strap around her belly and fix her to the shed so she can't move,' which is probably a modern equivalent of tying the back legs. 'Tie a dog in the shed and she'll be so keen to protect the calves from the dog she won't notice the calves suckling.' Eventually honey is the consensus answer. 'Put some honey on your fingers and let the calves suck it off then put some honey on the cow's teats and the calves will be mad after it.' There's much nodding of heads in agreement. Which is disappointing as they've missed the point, the calves are keen enough to suckle, it's the cow that won't let them. My advice to her next time she comes is to rear the calves on the bucket and sell the cow and buy another one. Which is what she has already decided to do. Rough justice, tough love, whatever, the cow's only got herself to blame. The reality was that it was the cow that needed the honey not the calves.

★★★

It's a busy time of year. 'Things' happen on a daily basis. The keeper shot a fox. Not that remarkable in itself but I think it was the fox that was killing our poultry, because we've left a dead chicken in a fox trap on the yard and it is untouched. Where we live is on the edge of going up into what they call marginal land, that is, a step towards hill country. Farmers on this marginal land report the best lambing weather they can remember, but they qualify that by saying that they have lost more lambs to predators this year than they have to the weather. Farmers are good moaners (you might have noticed this), but losing lambs to predators is heart-breaking. Foxes are the main culprit around here: a determined fox will soon separate one lamb from a set of twins and confuse the ewe, and before the ewe knows what's happened, there's a lamb gone.

Next on the list are ravens, a problem that is getting worse each year. Ravens like eyes, they like eyes almost as much as they like tongues. A lamb without a tongue soon dies because it can't suckle. But it's not all bad news; there's some good (lest you should think me a moaner as well). We've caught five magpies and my favourite wild cat in our magpie trap. I don't know how many fledgling songbirds five magpies will kill every day but I can be sure it's made a difference. My favourite cat is a favourite because it is a beautiful all-over grey colour. Where the colour came from I don't know. Releasing a feral cat from a magpie trap is something to be undertaken with caution and preferably with strong gloves, and a feral cat newly-released from a trap and making a dash for freedom is a sight to behold.

★★★

My cockerel has sorted out his sexuality issues and can be heard crowing every morning as it gets light. He lives with the turkeys and I think they intimidate him. He's got ten pullet wives who stroll about with the turkeys with impunity but the cockerel always lives around the boundaries of their enclosure and he only crows when he's out of sight behind some nettles. And the good news just keeps on coming. We've got a turkey hen sitting on 18 eggs in the nettles. (Well-off for nettles, us.) I rushed into the kitchen, 'The turkeys have started to hatch'. 'Whatever do you want more turkeys for?' 'Well, we'll need one for Christmas dinner.'

31 MAY 2014

I've been on a week's holiday so I suppose I'd better tell you about it. I've been to St Ives which is a long way from here. That in itself is not a problem because I like driving and in particular I like driving my Jag. Jaguars are supposed to provide space, pace and grace, and they do. Mine is really smooth, but not quite as smooth as me. So I was looking forward to driving to Cornwall and was more than a little annoyed that it developed a bit of a knock three days before we went. It wasn't a mechanical knock, it was more of a 'when you go over a bump sort of knock'. I had passengers in the car a couple of times before we went and I asked them if they could hear it. They all said that compared with their cars, it was really quiet and they couldn't hear a thing. But I could hear it and it bothered me. It bothered me because I had a long way to go and it was getting too late to get booked in anywhere to have something done about it. Then I discovered that if I put the radio on I couldn't hear it. So that solved the problem. Mustn't make life too difficult. We were going as a sort-of collective family, self-catering in a rental cottage. The women put so much food in the car the seagulls followed us all the way from the Severn Bridge to Cornwall. My brother was driving the other car, he's a retired headmaster so he thinks he's a lot brighter than me. We were starting out from different locations so I said I'd see him down there. He wanted to meet somewhere for coffee and drive the rest of the way in convoy. Anything for a quiet life, so I said OK, we'll meet at Taunton Deane services. He says, 'How will I know when we get there?' I said, 'There's a big blue sign on the side of the road that says "Taunton Deane".' 'Which side of the road is it?' 'On the left.' (Give me strength.) I said, 'The E on the end of Deane is silent,' for further clarity.

We didn't fall out until the Wednesday. My brother and sister are both artists and love going in art shops and galleries. Have you ever seen how many of those there are in St Ives? I seemed to be spending my week standing outside them. They didn't get the point until I stopped the car next day to look at a fine herd of Guernsey cows.

I love seafood and I'd never had lobster so I bought two from a fishmonger who cut them up for me. One was all beautiful and white and the other bright green. I asked what the difference was, she said, 'I've hit a sac with the knife but it's fine to eat, it will wash off under the tap.' Most of it did, it was all eaten, but I was just a bit worried. But it was a bit like the man in the Falklands war. I counted them out after it was eaten and I counted them back in for breakfast and they were all still there, no harm done. The only slight disappointment of the whole holiday was that I didn't see the camel on the M5. It's been a landmark for our family as we've gone on holiday in the West Country for years and years. 'Look out for the camel,' has been known to keep bored young children quiet for 20 to 30 miles.

★★★

Not many days after I returned from holiday, *Western Daily Press* sent out a photographer to take some fresh photographs of me. I was very pleased actually, some that they have used lately make me cringe. Years ago I had to have a 'serious' photograph taken that showed me sitting at a desk. I had to put a suit and tie on for the occasion and as we finished, the photographer says, 'I'll take a couple outside.' So without thinking I put my overalls on but inadvertently left the tie on, which I think looks really stupid. Anyway I'm doing my jobs earlier in the morning and when I'm feeding the turkeys, the three stags launch a ferocious attack on me. I think that would make a good photograph for a newspaper. So when the photographer comes, we go into the turkey pen but the turkeys completely ignore me and chase the photographer, which wasn't what we were looking for. Anyway he takes lots of other photos around the farm. It's not as easy as you think, you have to give more thought to the background than the actual photograph content. Who wants to have a nice photograph taken of you stroking the dog if, in the background there is a shed that looks as if it is about to fall down or a field full of docks and nettles! Either background is easy to find here. So photographs taken, he gets ready to go. I offer him some photographs taken of me in my early 30s, but he's not interested. Pity, that.

★★★

There's quite a lot of oil seed rape grown around here and I know several people who say that they don't like the bright yellow colour. The flowers are dying off this week and the fields are returning to green. And as this happens, the old meadows in the area, of which there are also quite a lot, are turning bright yellow as the buttercups come into flower. Strange therefore that the people who are saying to me, 'Isn't it nice to see those yellow fields of buttercups?' are the same people who didn't like the yellow oil seed rape?

7 JUNE 2014

In the last month, and all within a radius of about five miles, I know of six farms that have gone down with TB. And those are the ones I know about, I am sure there will be more because some farmers try to keep it secret, as if there is a stigma to having TB. This is a shame because there is almost nothing that they can do to prevent an outbreak, and it would be better if all their neighbours knew so they could take action to prevent spread. Just putting up an electric fence ten yards away from a boundary that will stop cattle 'kissing' each other over the fence would be a very effective precaution. What is clear is that things around here are getting worse and there is absolutely nothing going on to rectify the problem. What is unclear, in a week of political upheaval, is what will happen after next year's general election. TB will be at the bottom of most parties' agendas at the moment. In the meantime, and for the foreseeable future, cattle will continue to go for slaughter and the waste will go on.

★★★

There was a fire, so the story goes, a fire in an isolated, semi-derelict,cottage, many years ago. Semi-derelict means half fallen down, not that that matters, because the man who lives in it only lives in half of it anyway. There used to be lots of these cottages dotted about the countryside around here a couple of generations ago. They would have been for shepherds or forestry workers and most of them fell down just before a pile of stones could get planning permission for renovation into holiday homes or the like. You still come across these piles of stone in woods or the corner of fields and wonder to yourself what sort of isolated life it was for the people who lived and raised families there. Anyway, back to the fire, the local fire brigade are on their way there and the firemen are discussing the fire and the occupant. The consensus of all the scraps of information that they piece together is that it comprises a scullery and a living room downstairs and a landing and one bedroom upstairs. That the man who lives there hasn't been upstairs for years because the floorboards aren't safe. (This is very important fireman-information.) They know that the man who lives there doesn't have a bathroom (and looks like it), and that his facilities are at the bottom of the garden, unless it is snowing or raining, when he uses the sink. His water is carried from a well, occasionally. And he sleeps in an old armchair by the fireplace in a room that he fills with firewood up to the armchair. And he shares all this with six or seven dogs.

None of the firemen says so but there is certainly a mutuality of feeling that no one should risk life or limb saving this cottage. When they get there, there is lots of smoke but not a lot of flame. The resident is outside trying to stop the dogs from biting the firemen and protesting innocence of what had happened. 'I went to sleep in the chair reading the paper, next thing I know there's smoke everywhere,' he says. He is unaware that there is a fragment of cigarette paper sticking to his bottom lip. One of the younger keener firemen volunteers to go inside to see what is going on. The smoke is dense up to the ceiling so he gets down onto his hands and knees and crawls forward in the small space of clear air that there is. In covering about three yards he puts his hands into dog mess four times. He crawls back the way he has come and out of the front door. 'Well?' asks the head fireman. 'Let her go,' he replies.

★★★

A friend of mine is making her way slowly and carefully, even gingerly, into the world of IT. To start with, a few weeks ago, she knew even less about it than I did. But she's bought herself an iPad and she's doing quite well. High on her list of priorities, in this new world, are online shopping and Facebook. These two activities will take her ahead of me as I have no intention of ever doing either. So she finds out that to be on Facebook she needs a picture profile. 'How do I do that?' she asks her family. 'I'll do that for you, Mum,' says her teenage son. 'Isn't he a good boy,' she thinks to herself, and tells all her friends. Then one of her friends phones her up. 'Have you seen your picture profile on Facebook?' She hasn't so she has a look. There's a picture on there of a bottle of beer and a dead squirrel.

14 JUNE 2014

It wasn't formally planned but people around here seem to have made a concerted effort against the magpie population. Traps have been deployed everywhere and a rough count amongst the people I know would take the birds culled to over 60. That's a lot of magpies in a relatively small area. That's a population seriously out of balance! Everyone was motivated by the distressing sight of magpies pillaging the nests of songbirds for eggs and fledglings.

★★★

One of our charity fundraisers at the pub is called a 'Sweet and Savoury Evening'. The idea is for people to bring along a sweet or savoury dish, or both. You pay £5 to enter and when all the dishes are present, you go around, sample the dishes and vote on them. Some people don't bring anything with them but pay £5 to 'graze' the dishes. As organiser there is a fine line here between having enough entries to allow for the grazers and having enough food to satisfy them. You don't have to be a genius to work out that £5 is a very cheap evening meal which isn't really in the spirit of the charity, but we usually manage to get £5 out of them for the raffle. But then we wouldn't have a raffle if it weren't for the people who bother to make a dish also bringing the raffle prizes! Anyway, to move on, last year I made a prawn curry. I told the landlady of the pub how I'd made it and she said 'You're not bringing that here, it will kill everybody.' She worried me so much I tried it on myself, it didn't kill me and on the evening people said much nicer things about it. This year I was a bit more cautious and made a Thai chicken curry. I chuck in what I fancy and I buy the curry paste in the shop and that's it. So I try it first on my two eldest grandsons. I can't tell you what they said but they both went for glasses of water. I thought it was nice and tasty, with a violent afterburn. So I'm a bit worried and I take a sample to the pub at midday. I ask her what she thinks. I didn't realise she was so religious! 'How much curry paste did you put in?' 'Two jars.' 'You're only supposed to put in two tablespoons!' So I dash off to the shops and fetch two more tins of coconut milk and put that in there as well. That succeeds in taking the sting out of it a bit, but it can still take you by surprise.

So I sprinkle some coriander leaves on it and off we go. And I won! Won by a bit of a distance in fact. People kept asking me for the recipe. 'Sorry I can't, it's an old family recipe.' Like I look as if I come from an old Thai family! So there we are, we make over £200 on the night, and a very pleasant way of making £200 it was too. We had enough food, but only just. I was really chuffed to win, as there were some serious cooks there. But that was not the end of it, that particular week. Yet another accolade was to fall on my shoulders. The week ended up being quite special. Accolades don't very often fall on dairy farmers. What mostly falls on dairy farmers usually comes from under a cow's tail. The following Sunday I was asked to transport the mayor of our local town, in my Jag, from the Town Hall to the church in the parade that marks Mayor's Sunday. And back again after the service. It's up on a steep hill. That's two brides and a lady mayor I've had in my Jag now – it's opening up a whole new social life.

21 June 2014

I empathised with a recent piece in *West Country Life* about the farmer who would not allow his TB reactor cows to undergo a long journey to slaughter. Good for him. It's double standards once again. There's a host of people who aspire to tell us how to look after our animals on the farm and then when those animals are under their jurisdiction, there are no standards at all. I won't let cows go from here unless I know how far they will have to go, even if finding out costs me money. But now it's even worse than I thought. I want my animals to have a good life whilst they are here and then as humane an end as is possible. I can't even be sure of that anymore. For all I know they could be ending their lives undergoing ritual slaughter without stunning. All driven by the money it costs to segregate carcases. What a disgrace.

★★★

There's quite a large lay-by outside the secondary school in our small local town: it's where the buses park to disgorge students (we don't have school children any more do we?) but the lay-by changes on Thursdays when the school is on holiday. Why? Well there are no buses there for obvious reasons and Thursdays are market days at the local livestock market which, unusually, is still situated within the town. So what changes? Well the lay-by is taken over by people from the Department of Transport, Trading Standards and the like. Their purpose is to pull in passing traffic, mostly farmers, to do every vehicle check known to man, to check what fuel they are using (there's rich pickings to be had checking for red diesel!), tax, MOT and insurance, animal movement, you name it. I don't know where the people come from who man the checkpoint, probably from an urban background, but it's probably also certain that they've never seen anything like us!

We farmers are a resourceful species, we contend with the vagaries of weather and animals on a daily basis. The first time this check occurred something like 180 vehicles were examined and nearly 100 prosecutions were instigated. Then the numbers died off. Mobile phones were busy, although this is not a good reception area. One of the main problems, or advantages, depending on whether you are a farmer or an inspector, is that there is quite a long straight before you get to the crossroads by the secondary school, so as you approach you can see all this activity in the distance. And there are escape routes to be had. Take a smart turn to the right and there is the local vets or a builders merchants, both of which have room to negotiate a 360° turn with Land Rover and trailer and head off back to the hills and safety. But that only worked for a short while. Enter the scene, four or five police motorbikes, who cruise the area and gather up these escapees and return them for scrutiny. Sometimes they will wait at the vets and accumulate three or four vehicles before they take them on. And isn't it just a splendid irony that the authorities are using just the same technique to gather farmers, that those same farmers use to gather their own sheep? It's very much like *One Man and His Dog* only the 'dogs' in question are burly policemen on BMW motorbikes. The latest ruse used by stopped farmers is to say that the wife has just phoned to say there's a cow at home having a really difficult calving, that I'm to drop these sheep off at market and get home immediately, if you hold me up here for half an hour, will you take responsibility for the life of the cow and calf? This really tests them and thus far is working quite well but it will only be a matter of time before the inspectors think it is a coincidence that everyone has a cow calving at the same time, and call somebody's bluff.

I was talking to a farmer the other day, he says, 'I had a lucky escape last Thursday. I was taking a ewe to the vets that I couldn't lamb, in the Land Rover, and about 300 yards away all these trucks and trailers escorted by two police motorbikes pulled out and drove away. I only use the Land Rover on the road two or three times a year to go to the vets, saves making a mess of the back of the car. So it isn't worth taxing it or MOTing it, is it? She (it's a female Land Rover) hasn't got any insurance or lights or wing mirrors. Boy, that was lucky.' Now I will be the first to concede that running an illegal vehicle on the road is totally irresponsible, you wouldn't want to be in an accident with one, would you? But having said that, there is just a little tiny part of me that has a bit of sympathy with the people out there living happy, contented lives, in all other respects law-abiding and worthy but who manage to slip under the net of authority. That there is an undeniable logic that says it is not worth spending money on a Land Rover when 'I only use her on the road two or three times per year.' It just seems strange that most of those people seem to be living around here.

28 JUNE 2014

When I first came to live around here, I was a stranger, everything was new to me. And there were lots of decisions to make about the basics in my life. Things like where to get your hair cut, which pub to go in, where to play rugby. My wife had lived around here all her life so she knew the answers to all these questions but she could make an answer sound like an instruction and when you are newly-married there are important parameters to set down, one of which is to do as little as possible of what your wife tells you. Besides, I like to think that I have always been independent of spirit. There was a General Election soon after I arrived here, and this was very Blue country in those days, so I stuck a Liberal poster on a tree. It was pulled down within three hours and ever since I've been viewed with political suspicion as a sort of reactionary communist whose views were just to the left of Lenin. It annoys me a bit because when I vote I will examine all the issues and vote accordingly, but there's a part of me that likes the notoriety.

Anyway after I'd been around here about twelve months, I needed a dentist. Funny things, dentists. Why do they always try to make conversation when they've got their fists in your mouth? One of our bridesmaids became a dentist and she looked after my teeth for years. I think she used to do it a bit cheaper because when she was at school I used to give her hay for her pony. But she always made my appointment for 12.15pm and made me take her to lunch afterwards so it wasn't cheap at all. She's retired now and I hadn't been lately but eventually I made an appointment with her successor. I didn't realise she's been retired for three years! 'How can I help you?' 'I've got two fillings have come out and I need some plaque removing.' So she sits me down, pulls my mouth about for a quarter of an hour then says, 'You need two fillings and some plaque removing.' Right. But she's not doing any of that now, I'm to come back in six weeks' time! I can nearly see the £ signs in her eyes. Anyway, I've been jumping about a bit, let's get back to the story.

All those years ago I tell my wife I've got toothache: 'We always go to Mr Owens.' It's one of those instructions again. But I'd heard of this other dentist. His main claim to fame was that when he was younger he would go around the pubs at night looking for patients and remove their teeth in the pub for drink. This would involve a couple of the patient's friends holding him down in a chair and the dentist would kneel on his chest while he pulled the tooth out. I'd also heard the story of a farming family up in the hills who were the last, by some distance, to cut their corn with a binder to produce sheaves. (I told you this was an old story.) This binder was the old father's pride and joy and he wouldn't let his sons drive the tractor that pulled it, only he could do that.

One harvest the father was afflicted by a terrible toothache and progress with the binder was very slow, so the sons sent a message via the postman (no phone) for the dentist to attend. Which he duly did. He turned up in the cornfield and the sons and the dentist got the old man down on the bed of the binder and the offending tooth was removed. They reckoned there was a big patch of dried blood going round and round on the canvas of the binder and that you could still see it two harvests later when they swopped the binder for a combine. This was clearly the dentist for me, so I gave him a ring.

The phone call was a bit like that old joke about Newport County Football Club. A man phones up the club to ask if there's a match today. 'Yes.' 'What time is kick-off?' 'What time can you make it?' I phone the dentist and he asks where I live, so I tell him, 'Shall I say in a quarter of an hour then?' He lives and works in a private house on the edge of town and his surgery is one of the bedrooms. He is clearly overjoyed to have a new client (any client) and we make our way upstairs. There are a few sets of discarded false teeth on the stairs and lots of those white impressions they take when people are having a new set. But not as many as there are all over the surgery floor. I start to get a sense of foreboding, perhaps having an independence of spirit is not such a good idea after all.

With sideways sweeping movements of his feet he clears a pathway through this debris to the chair, which is clearly a museum piece. I sit down while he busies himself in preparation and I take in my surroundings. The drill is driven by a system of pulleys and cords that don't do anything for my confidence but I don't have time to dwell on that because before I know it he's kneeling over me, one knee between my legs, with a syringe in his hands. Most dentists work from behind your head. Lady dentists will sometimes cushion your head between their boobs (which is OK by me – is that sexist?). The injection, when it comes, is not as bad as I thought, not that I had much choice in the matter. 'We'll give that five minutes,' he says and proceeds to examine the bit on the drill. He switches it on and tests it for sharpness by making holes in a leather settee, which has so many holes in it, it looks as if someone has been practising darts on it. I get a new filling and it's OK. When my wife tells people where I've been to the dentist, they regard me with awe and I become a sort of hero. But if someone asks me about dentists I say, 'We always go to Mr Owens.'

5 July 2014

So I'm driving gently along the lanes on my daily rounds and at about 100 yards in front of me I can see two partridges in the road. I slow down to give them time to move but as I get nearer I see that one of them is dead, run over, and its mate can't work out what has happened. It has a bewildered air about it. 'Come on, there's a truck coming.' But there's no reaction and it, the live one, pops over the hedge out of my way. When I come back ten minutes later, the live bird is back standing next to the dead one. I don't know if partridges have facial expressions but its demeanour is that of sorrow and loss. Next morning the dead bird is gone, a meal for whatever scavenger, but there is still that lone partridge wandering about in the same place.

It's a sad story, well it made me sad anyway. There's actually no need to run these birds over on these narrow twisty lanes. A safe speed is to tootle along like I do at 20 mph but there's plenty of cars doing 50 (unless they get stuck behind me). At 20, wildlife and humans can get out of the way, unless they do something stupid. I was driving home from the pub last night and a hare loped across the road about 50 yards in front of me, crossing from one gateway to another. I said, 'Good night, Sarah' (a lot of people round here call hares Sarah, apparently regardless of its sex, which presumably they don't know). It must have been a female hare because, having crossed the road, it changed its mind completely and dashed back across the road in front of me. It was so close I couldn't see it in front of the bonnet. That would have been another sad story.

12 JULY 2014

They've gone now but there have been 17 lapwings up on our top ground for over a month. Because they've gone I'm assuming that they haven't bred. There could be lot of reasons for this, it could be me, we've had ground up there to work down and we've been on the lookout for eggs all the time, but if you spot them it is really good luck. The best guide we have is the behaviour of the birds. I've been off the tractor lots of times looking for eggs but never found any. But then I'm the least of their problems: there are buzzards, kites, ravens, carrion crows everywhere, never mind foxes and badgers at night. I'll never forget when I first left school and went to work on a farm, I spotted two lapwing eggs when I was ploughing a field. It was easier in those days, little grey Fergie tractor, no cab, close to the ground. So I moved those two eggs from where they were on the unploughed ground and set them down in a little depression I had made in the ground that was freshly ploughed. I moved on with my ploughing but noted that the lapwings returned to the eggs very quickly. After ploughing I probably disced the field twice, harrowed it twice, then drilled the kale. With each operation I would stop the tractor and move the eggs to a safe place and throughout the process I could see that the birds continued to sit their eggs. The last operation after drilling the seed was to roll the ground down.

So there I was rolling away and my thoughts probably miles away on some farmer's daughter when I stopped dead. Eggs! The two eggs were lying broken about 5 yards behind the roller. I was mortified, still am come to that. But we should always learn from our mistakes and that lesson taught me to push a stick into the ground as a marker, not too close to the eggs lest it disturbs the birds, but as a reminder to the distracted tractor driver.

I've employed the practice successfully dozens of times over the years since that first mishap and I know that most farmers do the same. I often hear them say in the pub: 'My two lapwing eggs have hatched out'. I doubt if my lapwings would have reared chicks successfully up on my top land. It's high and it's dry. As I understand it, lapwing chicks need to drink water within 24 hours of being hatched, that's why people manufacture little pools or scrapes for the chicks to drink. If there are lapwings up there next year, prior to the breeding season, I will put some places in for them to drink. I have a friend who farms a couple of miles away on much lower land, who has had 20 lapwings on his fields for over six months, that's really good news, the chances are that they have bred there, plenty of places to drink.

★★★

My memory isn't brilliant on some things but then again it completely confounds me with some of the detail I remember from many years ago. But without calling on my memory too much, I can't, off-hand, remember a worse two weeks within my life than the last two. Whoever planned Wimbledon to coincide with the soccer world cup? Who contrived the fact that the two events took place in different time zones so that the one event could follow the other, endlessly? I don't have to watch either, we have a television in the kitchen but we don't have satellite television in the kitchen, the chairs are harder in the kitchen and who wants to spend their lives in the kitchen? I like watching TV. I like watching films. I'm in love with Julia Roberts but that's another matter. The very worst scenario of all is women's tennis: all that squealing! If the kitchen door is open, and it usually is, even the dogs slink off up the yard when the squealing starts. Perhaps I should record it and incorporate it in a bird scarer. It falls, the squealing, somewhere between the sound of a sow stuck under a gate and a seagull with its foot caught.

26 July 2014

There's an old farmer I know, lives in Wiltshire, he phones up to comment on my tale about marking lapwings nests so that you don't break the eggs whilst cultivating a field. He tells me that when he was a student on a farm, they were expected to spend time sitting in the bottom of a hedge and watching for lapwings to land on a field. Lapwings will always land some distance from the nest and run to it. As they squatted down they would disappear but if you selected a marker in the opposite hedge and walked a straight line, you would come to the nest and could mark it.

★★★

It's agricultural show time. Every week the farming press carry reports and pictures of prize-winners. People in agriculture identify with their local show and are usually very proud of it. There's a lot of hard work goes into a show, whether a show flourishes or declines invariably rests on the people involved and the quality and dedication of those people. But it is usually a labour of love and what you get out of it is in proportion to what you put in. Bit like life itself. Amongst all the reports and pictures, pictures of the bovine equivalent of Miss West Country or possibly an ovine (sheep) Miss M5, there are reports of prime stock classes of sheep and cattle. These are often sold on into the meat trade at goodly prices and the purchaser will have the prize-winning rosette to display on his premises. Often, these days, the purchasing abattoir is a ritual slaughter one. I wonder what the vendors think about the animal they have bred and pampered ending up in a place like that. I wonder how ritual slaughter has ended up as an accepted norm in our society.

★★★

So we are chatting away in the pub and one man tells us that years ago he used to go to a pub a few miles away and when there were just a few of them there on winter evenings, they would have competitions to see who could tell the biggest lies. This gets absolutely no reaction from the rest of the audience except that I am thinking that we should start similar competitions here, as there would be some very good competitors. The conversation moves on and the man who made the original statement goes quiet. And there's me, once again thinking, this time I'm thinking, 'Wait for it'.

And here it comes. He's waited for his chance. 'I was out in the garden early one morning before breakfast, digging, and I could hear the geese coming back from the stubbles.' So far it's a feasible story. There are large lakes near here, home to hundreds of Canada geese. It's amazing how they know when the combines have started up, as soon as there are cleared corn fields in the area they will fly off in early evening and spend the night on the stubble feeding on spilt grain. Sometimes, but rarely, they will identify a

field where the corn has been battered down by the weather and go
to feed on that but I don't think they feel as safe there from foxes. A
cleared field gives foxes less opportunity to sneak up and even then
you can see ganders posted out as sentries.

Back to the story. 'I can hear the geese coming so I put my
fork down and go into the house to fetch the gun.' His audience is
spellbound, thus far the story is perfectly feasible. 'I come out into
the garden and my next-door neighbour sees me and says: "You'll
never get one of them, look how high they are." And they were
high, just tiny dots in the sky, but nevertheless I took aim, they
were flying back in a perfect V shape and I shot at one of those at
the back as you should always shoot at them: the oldest geese are at
the front and they are always tougher to eat.

'Bert next door says, "Told you they were too high," but
I say, "We'll wait and see." So I take the gun back into the house
and clean it and put it back in the cabinet and go back out into the
garden. Bert next door says, "Hang on, one of those dots is getting
bigger." And it was, it had gone from being a dot to something
a lot bigger. And on it comes. It had its wings half folded like
one of those gannets you see on the telly diving for fish and it
was making a whistling noise like one of those Stuka dive bombs
from WWII. It hit the roof of my cottage at a hell of a speed and
went straight through. It went through the bedroom ceiling, the
missus was still in bed, and it frightened the life out of her, straight
through the bedroom floor it went and ended up smack in the sink
in the kitchen, ready for her to feather when she got up.' His story
is finished and the end of it is greeted with much laughter and cries
of 'Liar!' Of course it was lies, they've missed the point of it all.

2 AUGUST 2014

I like looking at people and that's fair enough because I quite like
them looking at me. Once a week I take two of my grandchildren
to school. There's a secondary school and a primary school on the

same site. As far as I can make out, the primary school is in a sort of compound. The gates are locked until 8.45 then you take the child in all the way to the classroom, all the teachers are in the classrooms by then, and you sort of hand the child over. Which is in itself a sad indictment of the times we live in. Out in the car park it's mostly young mums bringing their children in, but I don't know if it was because it was the last day of term, there were a lot of dads as well. It's a lovely sunny morning and all the dads, nearly all, have a sort of uniform on. They are all wearing sunglasses, T-shirts, shorts and flip-flops. (Except for the two who have socks and sandals on, less said about them the better).

Then there's me. Apart from being a generation older, I haven't got sunglasses, but I'm wearing a T-shirt and shorts, I haven't shaved for a couple of days and I'm wearing thick working socks and heavy working boots. And they are all staring at me. Probably because they think they are cool, whereas I clearly am not. When I come back out, the dads are having a bit of a chat and I can see that they are looking at my Jag. It stands out a bit amongst all the sensible family cars, there's been heavy rain in the night so it's positively gleaming. Then to completely confound them, this tramp that they have just seen taking a little boy into school gets into the Jag and drives away in it. I look in the mirror and can see them all watching. I quite like people looking at me.

★★★

I'm late for the pub one Thursday night. All this soccer on the television had made *Coronation Street* a bit late and I always like to watch that. Some people think they are all actors, but they are not, they are real people living real lives. I used to have a picture of Tina, who has just been murdered, on my phone screen. She was in the pub one Christmas and I had a picture taken of her sitting on my knee, but I dumped her when she started two-timing me. Anyway, I'm late for the pub so when I turn up the conversation is already in full flow. There's a brief pause while they shuffle around to make room for me on the settle and one of the younger ones fetches a stool. I don't like sitting with my back to the room, I've had a tough life, where I come from you can't turn your back for a second. The conversation continues where it left off. 'If you have a bucket full of rats,' and I wonder to myself what had started this off, but best not interrupt. But you can't help wondering can you? They all nod their heads around the table, knowingly, as if having a bucket full of rats was a commonplace occurrence in their lives. 'You can take them out one at a time and they'll never hurt you, until you get to the last one, boy you must never touch the last one, he'll have you.' And they all nod in agreement, all except me, who is completely bemused by the whole episode. Think I'll have to start recording *Coronation Street* in future.

But that was not the end of rat stories, it turns out to be a ratty sort of week. There's a bachelor farmer living alone up in the hills near here, on an isolated farm. Someone had seen him at market. 'Saw old Jones last week, he was selling lambs. He was telling me he had been bitten by a rat on his leg and on his finger while he was in bed.' It's always me that wants more detail. 'Was he actually in the bed or was he lying on top?' 'He didn't say.' And the storyteller scowls at me for interrupting. To me the detail is very important, there's a huge difference in the two scenarios. Were the rats running about on top of the bed or were they running about within the bed? I worked on a farm once where my bedroom was in an outbuilding, there were rats running about on the floor all night. I've never been scared of rats but shall I say I didn't get the best of night's sleep. They put some poison down the next day and that was the end of that. 'The rats won't trouble him again.' 'Why not?' It's me again and I get another scowl. 'Because he's started sleeping in a chair in the kitchen and all his dogs live in the kitchen.' And my mind works overtime again and I picture this scenario of this man who has, to all intents, abandoned his bedroom to the rats. What will happen if he forgets to let the dogs in one night?

16 August 2014

You get a lot of flies around farms. I suppose that if you look at it from a fly's point of view, a farm isn't a bad place to hang out. There's all that poo and stuff about. But if you are a fly you don't always draw a distinction between farm and house. So you get a lot of flies around the farm and invariably in the house as well. We put fly repellent on the cattle, we give them a garlic flavoured-compound that they can lick which is supposed to repel flies. In the milking parlour we don't mess about. There's electric zappers and buckets of horrible stuff that will kill any fly that comes near it. Flies biting cows at milking time can cause some of the worst milking sessions of the year.

So we turn to the house. Our big old farmhouse is nice and cool in hot weather (freezing in the winter but that's life), but we get flies in the kitchen, probably because the kitchen door is always open. (We also get dogs, hens, turkeys in the kitchen, probably because the door is always open.) Our main defence against flies is the use of those old-fashioned sticky flypapers. And they are OK, up to a point. I mostly breakfast alone, sad, I know, but alone can be OK, and I don't need to wait around for my breakfast, waiting for all the flies to land on the sticky paper. So once a day, I have a bit of a fly clear-out. I shut doors and windows and give the kitchen a blast with an aerosol. For reasons that are unclear this is not very popular with the ladies that run the house. They like to see the flies on the sticky paper: it must be down to a vindictive element of their nature. So we proceed with our fly battle as an uneasy compromise. But because the kitchen door is otherwise always open, we get other things in our kitchen. Sometimes we get fledgling birds that have lost their way. Mostly they find their way back out again, sometimes they need help.

Last week I came into the kitchen and there was a wren in here. There's been a colony of wrens living in the bushes outside our front door for years. This wren needed a bit of help returning to the wild. It was stuck firmly to the flypaper. I used to feed these wrens in winter but have let it lapse. It's gone back on my list of things to do.

***

We had the old kitchen garden wall fall down. Ivy, frost, water, won the day. We had to knock all the rest down, tidy it all up with a JCB and put a new fence up to replace the wall. It meant that we ended up with an extra area that I could sow down to more lawn. It is a hard piece of ground and I intended to buy some top soil to put on top of it to put grass seed in. But my milk price has gone down four pence per litre thus far this year and I don't need to be buying anything that I can manage without, so I scratched the grass seed in as best I could. About 75% grew and it doesn't look too bad, from a distance. Lawns equal moles here and they have already found the new piece of lawn. This morning there were three molehills on it. Three molehills of the finest crumbly soil that you could wish for. Where, I ask myself, did they find such lovely soil amongst all that hard rocky sub-soil?

***

Everything in life is relative. It's a favourite saying of mine. So what's an example? Well we've had floods, floods that have had a huge negative impact on people's lives. But we don't get floods that go for hundreds of miles and displace thousands. We don't get the sort of torrential mountain-slides that bury hundreds of people. So that's an extreme example but relatively speaking 'our' floods are not worse than theirs. Here's another example. I've just met a really nice Chinese lady. She originates from a village in China. You could describe the village as primitive but that sounds a bit derogatory and I don't mean it to be so I will say that is was basic. When she first came to this country she went to school to learn English, she had to get work in the evenings to survive and throughout her time here, people have marvelled at her tremendous work ethic. Today she is married with two young children, teaches in a university and after a really busy day thinks nothing of producing a splendid Chinese meal for ten or twelve people. Someone said to her recently 'How do you manage to work so hard?' 'I don't work hard, that's not hard work. In the past I've had to pull the plough when the oxen was sick. Now that's hard work.' I've never pulled a plough myself, never had to, but relatively speaking, I bet that is really hard work. I don't think that any of us has to dig too far into that story to find one of life's lessons.

23 August 2014

They call it the migration of the middle classes, away from the major supermarkets to the discounters. The loss of business that is a result of that is causing big issues for the four big-name retailers, whilst the discounters seem to go from strength to strength. It's not for me to give the impression that we, in some way, belong to the middle classes. I've never been under any illusion that I come from the wrong side of the tracks (I come from the wrong side of the tracks wherever you should choose to build them), but the shopper in this house has made the same shopping journey. So we are having this daily post mortem. 'Who has been eating those baked beans?' 'Me.' 'What were they like?' 'Fine.' 'That's good, they were half the price of the beans we usually buy.' 'Who has been eating those tinned tomatoes?' 'Me.' 'Were they any good?' 'Just the same as we always have.' 'Good, they were a lot cheaper.'

But then we get to the bread. We've been having the same seeded brown loaf for years and I really like it, compared to what she's just been buying it's a mile better. 'How do you like the bread?' 'It's OK.' 'Good, it's £1 a loaf cheaper.' But here comes my masterstroke. 'But the boys (the two eldest grandsons, who are eating us out of house and home on a daily basis) don't like it a bit.' There's no comment, but we are back on the old bread straightaway, what's left of the new bread ends up as turkey food. I didn't get where I am today without a bit of cunning. Personally, and I'm not a vindictive person, I'm quite pleased to see one particular supermarket getting a bloody nose, they were getting much too big and powerful and having too great an influence on the country for anybody's good.

★★★

When our working farm dogs were bearded collies it was essential to clip their coats off every year. Their coats would get long and thick and by springtime there would be so much dried 'muck' hanging onto their fur, they would rattle as they walked about. It never crossed my mind to take them to a professional dog clipper, so I did it myself. So much cow clippers, so much with my wife's dressmaking scissors, a bit at a time, the length of the bits depending on my skill and the dog's patience. It would be a protracted process that could take over a week and the dogs would go through a process of clipping, a bit at a time, that would often leave them looking very much like the sheepdog on that Specsavers advert that I like. It had never crossed my mind to clip a more conventional breed of sheepdog like Mert but two years ago I took him to be clipped when someone suggested it after seeing him panting on a hot day. It was a revelation how it changed him. It took years off his demeanour; he became more active and clearly more comfortable.

For reasons that are not clear, and that I now regret, I didn't take him to be clipped last year. I think it got a bit late and I didn't want him to go into the winter without a warm coat. But he's been clipped this year and once again the change in him is a revelation, both in his appearance and in his behaviour.

He's an old dog now and spends most of the nights barking; I think he barks at badgers, foxes and the moon, if there is one. Now he's clipped there's a bit of the puppy back in his ways. He's gone back to chasing vans and biting their tyres (one went over his front leg but that has made him even more determined). He's gone back to threatening people and because he's slimmer, he's now more comfortable on the tractor with me.

Anyway, a couple of Sundays ago there was a vintage tractor
run around here. There are lots of vintage tractors enthusiasts around
here and they do regular 'runs' for charity. This particular run was
calling here for coffee and we were all up the yard waiting for them
to arrive. We were serving coffee in a shed (well you wouldn't
want them all in the house, would you?). It's quite a spectacle, this
convoy of vintage tractors, there were 51 of them that came up on
our yard and a lot of our neighbours had turned up to watch. There
wasn't much comfort to be had while we were waiting, so I was
sitting on my lawnmower and Mert was sitting at my side. We have
a neighbour who lives in a conversion on our yard (he actually sees
Mert every day). He comes up to me with his grandchildren and
says 'I've noticed you've got a new dog.' I confirm that this is so. So
he gives Mert a pat and a stroke and says 'What's his name?' And I
tell him that I call him Mert. 'Oh, that's a nice touch,' he says. So
he introduces Mert to his grandchildren, 'Look, this is Mert', and
Mert gets more pats and strokes. Then he comes up close and puts
his head close to my ear and asks, 'What happened to the old Mert?'
The conspiratorial whisper is presumably because he is expecting
some tale of Mert's untimely death in tragic circumstances that he
doesn't want his grandchildren to hear. I lean back towards him and
whisper, 'That's him, there.' His reply was something else he didn't
want his grandchildren to hear.

30 August 2014

I've told you that I live in a beautiful area. I've told you that I
consider myself lucky to be here. Visitors to the area frequently tell
me the same two things but they invariably qualify that by saying
that because I'm here every day, there is no way I can appreciate it.
I always resent them saying that because just as invariably I remind
myself how lucky I am every day. And because of all that love and
pride in our area, when someone dumps rubbish on verges and

lay-bys it makes me very angry. It's as if some sort of desecration has taken place. There are people about who fly tip professionally because they have been paid by someone to remove stuff from their premises and told them that the cost is based on what it will in turn cost them to dispose of whatever it is, legally. Then they fly tip it and put what they've charged in their back pockets. It's a win-win for them and a double fiddle. Disposing of waste should be cheap and easy but it's neither of these things. As a consequence of this, the 'authorities' are not without blame. It's not easy and it's not cheap, so you get fly tipping as a consequence but the authorities end up having the cost of clearing up the fly tipping, so it's a perpetual cycle of cost. There have been two examples of fly tipping around here lately. One was the almost obligatory pile of builders' waste dumped on a grass verge and the other, almost unbelievably, bones and slaughter waste dumped off a bridge into a stream. You have to wonder what sort of person would do that.

I have a friend who was moving house and who decided that his old settee and armchairs were now surplus to requirements. So he borrowed a small trailer and took them to the local tip, or should I say, recycling depot. So he pulls up in the yard at the appropriate place and two hi-vis yellow-clad men appear. 'Where do you think you are going with that?' Sensing difficulties already, this friend indicates the pile of household items (one that already contains settees and armchairs) and says, ever so politely, that he wants to add his furniture to the pile. 'Have you got a licence to bring that trailer in here?' He hadn't. 'Well if you haven't got a licence, you can't bring them in.' 'If I had an estate car, could I bring them in one at a time?' He is told that would be fine, but as he's got a trailer they can't help him. Less responsible people might have dumped the settee and armchairs on the grass on the side of a quiet lane on the way home and you would have to have some sympathy with that. But my friend is not irresponsible and he's a resourceful countryman. So he gets back in his car, drives back out of the gate, manoeuvres the furniture about on the trailer so that he can get each item in turn onto his back and carries them back into the recycling depot. Consternation! They try to stop him. What if you hurt yourself carrying that settee? Who will be responsible? What about health and safety? By the time they have finished flapping and fetching their manager, the furniture is dumped in the appropriate place and my friend is off home.

★★★

A friend of mine is having cavity wall insulation installed. He says I should have my walls done. Some chance. The only cavities that were about when they built our house were in people's teeth. Anyway, these three men turn up to do his walls and he's not particularly impressed with their demeanour, they seem much more interested in how long it will be before he makes them a cup of tea than in reducing his carbon footprint. They sort of hang about for a few minutes until he says he'll put the kettle on and there is action of a sort and they start to get ladders and kit out of their van. He makes a pot of tea and is just giving consideration to the idea that a few biscuits might be a good investment in the circumstances, when he sees ladders and kit going back towards the van. So he goes back outside to see what's going on and they tell him the job has been cancelled. Naturally he wants to know why and they tell him the job is too dangerous.

Once again he wants to know why, and they tell him that there's a wasps' nest under his eaves. This friend of mine isn't big on patience and he's starting to illustrate that with some of the language he's using. So he demands that they point out this blankety blank wasps' nest, telling them he hasn't seen a wasp for days. They take him to the rear of the house and point out a house martin's nest tucked under the eaves. He tells them what it is but they are unconvinced and say that they only have his word for it. He knows that the birds have fledged now so he says: 'Give me one of those ladders and I'll get it down.' But they won't lend him a ladder because they say he's not licensed to use it, health and safety. He can't use his own ladder because I'd borrowed it, so he has to go and borrow a neighbour's. Anyway, after all that, he gets the empty nest down, they drink the cold tea and start work. And my friend tells me the whole story very much as I have told it to you, but without the language.

6 SEPTEMBER 2014

The two eldest grandsons have just been to a pop festival for the weekend. I've never been to a pop festival so it is incumbent on me to interrogate them. It's what I call 'finding out'. If you don't ask questions of life, how do you learn about life at all? So I want to know all about it and, as far as I know, they tell me about it. I don't think they held much back because a couple of nights later they wanted a big favour of me, I had to take them in the middle of the night to catch a bus to Gatwick. Anyway we next get to drugs. I know very little about what goes on in the world of young people and drugs. I've never been offered drugs, probably because I'm a generation too old, but even I know where I can get them locally. Two young people died at this particular pop festival from taking 'drugs', and, according to which newspaper you read, hundreds had to go to hospital, so it seems reasonable to assume that lots were taken ill. The boys tell me that they were offered drugs frequently. 'Want some E's?' '£3 each or three for a tenner.' Which makes 'Buy one get one free' an amazing offer.

I don't know why but a story came to mind, a very old story, of two young lads who would cycle several miles on Saturday nights to visit two girls who lived in another village. The youths who lived in the village where the girls lived were very envious of the attentions these two lads were receiving and one Saturday night, emboldened by a few pints of cider, they took these lads bikes and threw them off the bridge into the river. They didn't do it very quietly and they didn't do it very well. Within half an hour everyone knew what had happened and who had done it, everyone included the village policeman. He soon rounded up the miscreants, took them down to the bridge and to the water's edge. The story goes that the river was in spate. The policeman wasn't a bit bothered about that. He sent the lads responsible into the river, fully clothed. To retrieve the bikes. The story also goes that the water was up to their chins, but as stories also go, it is fairly safe to assume that it was up to their waists, and we can be sure that it was cold and wet! So the bikes were retrieved. Those lads never threw a bike in a river again. It was rough justice but it was probably very effective. No one would dare to do something like that today. But a bit of rough justice is not without its merit. You can't help but think that the people who put young people's lives at risk by selling dodgy drugs could do with a dose of that, and perhaps a smack round the ear for those foolish enough to take them.

★★★

Despite an abundance of hen pheasants who survived the shooting season and went on to have the opportunity to breed and produce pheasants of their own, I have yet to see a single pheasant poult that they have reared. I told the keeper and he hasn't seen one either. But he's always got a story, has the keeper. He tells me that on another part of the estate, some partridges have hatched out some young, that they have all come together in a sort of super crèche and there is a group of chicks numbering 31 all told. Have you ever seen partridge chicks? They go about like a group of large bumblebees.

★★★

I love my grandchildren dearly. You've probably spotted that. Grandchildren are one of the very best things that ever happens to you in life. But, there's always a but, as they get older they get quite proficient with the TV remote control. You go to sit down in your armchair and find that they are glued to some endless USA teenage sitcom best described as crap. I look forward to watching programmes I have marked down to record but find that they haven't been recorded because the recorder is full of the life and times of someone with the unbelievable name of Hannah Montana! Yesterday we had a lovely evening, too nice for TV, 'Come on let's go round the cattle, there might even be some mushrooms.' (We'd had some heavy rain and the ground was nice and warm, so there could be mushrooms.) We only have one place that produces mushrooms and we drove slowly along it but not a mushroom was to be seen. 'No luck tonight,' I tell them. They are disappointed, they have bags ready and a penknife to cut them. Katie pipes up from the back. 'I expect it's because the ratio of moisture, temperature and light are not at the optimum for cell growth.' Mushrooming used to be such a simple practice.

13 SEPTEMBER 2014

I grow cereals of my own but they don't provide all the straw I need to bed down our livestock, so I buy straw off neighbours after they have combined their fields. It's a bit of a judgement call, how much you buy, and I always work on the criteria, better safe than sorry. So I hope to have plenty of straw in store and if it's too much, I can always sell some in the spring.

There's quite a lot of corn grown around here but there's a lot of demand for the straw, because there are a lot of hill livestock farms only a tractor and trailer ride away. I've got two neighbours who both sell me 40 acres of straw each, every year, but if I said I didn't want it one year and it was sold to someone else, I couldn't be sure of getting 'back in'. It also gives me flexibility. If grass silage crops are light I can cut a cereal crop of my own, while the grain is still a bit soft, and cut it, grain and straw into a silage pit, for cattle feed for the winter. We call it whole crop, you obviously lose the straw for bedding, but it doesn't matter because you've got some booked with your neighbour. I think I've explained that.

Anyway, we are into the catchy weather we've just had,

showers and sun on a daily basis, and my nephew, who is one of the neighbours who sells me straw, moves his combine into a 40 acresfield of wheat late morning. The straw is for us, it's a bright sunny day, good for the job, but in the distance you can see storm clouds tracking the hills.

So off he goes and after he's made a good start we phone for a contractor to come and bale the straw into those big square bales. Then Stephen comes with the loader and starts to put the bales into big stacks so that if it rains, most of the straw will be dry. Me, I'm sitting in the truck watching. The combine cuts 25ft at a time, the baler starts well behind but is catching up fast, and Stephen is keeping up with the baler. Fifty years ago the combine would have an 8ft 6-inch cut. The wheat would be dropped on the floor in 2cwt sacks and all the straw would be in little bales. A trailer would go around to collect the sacks of wheat and two men with a stick between them would get each sack in turn, stand it on its feet, then tilt the sack over the stick and together lift it up onto the trailer.

All the little bales were put onto trailers by hand with a pitchfork but straw bales were easy, lighter than hay. By nine o'clock all the corn is cut and in the barn. All the straw is baled and stacked up. I haven't been out of the truck except for a pee. Do I feel guilty? Not a bit. Fifty years ago it was me in the same field, doing all that lifting and carrying. It's the ones who have done the work today who have had it easy.

★★★

I went down to my daughter's the other day. They farm beef, sheep and corn. They were having a family day with their sheep. Dad, Mum and their two children, I think they were injecting their ewes. I didn't go to help them but waited in the house. You never know what stage of frustration the combatants will be at and where tempers will be when there's a lot of sheep work going on. If it had been me involved, I would have soon lost patience with their terrier, who wasn't allowed in the handling shed, but stood at the door, barking continuously. Half an hour of that would have been enough for me, never mind two or three hours. Eventually, job done, my daughter and her children join me in their kitchen. They are in quite good spirits despite being covered in what sheep do. My daughter tells me that there were only two swear words that the children didn't know and now they know those as well. The terrier is well pleased with himself and takes up his customary position on the windowsill with the air of someone who has injected all the sheep on his own. Very important little dogs, terriers.

I was telling this story to a friend of mine who tells me that his son has a terrier and one morning they were sorting lambs to take to market. They had two or three sheepdogs involved but the terrier was clearly in charge of the whole proceedings, especially the other dogs. He was into everything, into the pen, out of the pen, barking at the other dogs, actually a bit of nuisance. Eventually they had their lambs sorted and load them in the trailer and prepared to set off for market. The sheepdogs got into the back of the Land Rover, 'Now where's that bloody terrier?' 'It must have gone back to the house.' So off they go to market, back up to the pens, let down the tailboard, out come the lambs – plus the terrier – which is looking well pleased with himself and even more important than ever.

20 SEPTEMBER 2014

So I've just met this man who tells me that he has to take two live billy goats to London for an ethnic wedding of some sort. He won't tell me how much they will be worth when they get there and I don't know much about the worth of billy goats but it will be a day's driving and use a lot of fuel, so they can't be cheap. Many years ago I used to export game products to France and one day I drove the van to southwest Scotland to buy a load of frozen rabbits. It was to a place I hadn't been to before so I took what looked like the shortest route on the map. It might have looked the shortest route but it certainly wasn't the quickest. Uphill and down whatever they call downhill in Scotland, probably down the glen, it took hours. But I did notice quite a lot of wild goats on the hills. So when I eventually get to the man with the rabbits, I ask him 'What's with all those goats?' He tells me that he's had his eye on these goats for some time and thought that they could present a commercial opportunity. So he makes enquiries and eventually gets an order for a vanload of shot goats into London. So he goes out, and with some help shoots a vanload of billy goats. And off they go, early one morning, to find London and to seek their fortune. After an hour the smell was so bad they had to open the windows of the van. After two hours they had to drive with their heads out of the window. After two hours they still hadn't got to Carlisle and that's still a long way to go to London, especially with your head out of the window!

After the goats were unloaded they washed the van out but it was so bad they still had to drive back with the windows open. When they got back they had the inside of the van steam cleaned on three separate occasions but to no avail. 'So what did you do?' 'We had to sell the van.' There's probably a moral to this story, there's probably several morals. If you are a vegetarian you are probably thinking, 'Serves them right'. For the rest of us, we need to be careful if we are buying a second-hand van from the south of Scotland and should any of us get an order for billy goats for ethnic festivals in London, probably best to walk them there down old drovers' roads.

27 SEPTEMBER 2014

I've got several patches of root crops this year for cattle to eat in the winter. So here comes the keeper, 'Is it OK if I put some partridge pens on those roots?' I tell him he can. Then I lead him gently towards a topic. 'Will you be rearing any English grey partridge this year?' Grey partridge are lovely little birds that are in decline because of the activities of nasty farmers like me. There are incentives to increase the grey partridge population, and there is a lot of money being thrown at it, but we'll come to that later. You can buy grey partridge chicks commercially so that isn't a problem. So it's not a problem to source them, the problem is keeping them alive. I know that the keeper has been putting grey partridge down every year, that's why I asked the question. I can't give you his reply, there might be children reading this, so I'll translate the colourful language for you. This is the first year he hasn't reared greys for some years because they never survive the predation of buzzards and kites. Grey partridge instinctively squat down close to the ground when predators are about and are picked off by buzzards and kites like mushrooms. French partridge run for cover.

'People' tell me that kites are only scavengers but it's not true. We've just done our third cut silage and I've seen kites take three leverets whilst I've been on the tractor. I believe in evolution. It's a very simple principle. Species evolve and thus thrive. If they don't, they don't. Just ask any passing dodo. Vultures are scavengers. Some vultures have evolved that have beaks that can rip a carcase open. Some vultures have beaks that enable them to rip out entrails, and some vultures have beaks that can shave flesh off bones. If you watch them on TV they will queue up to take turns to do what they have evolved to do, because there's an order, a sequence to it all. That's evolution at work. If I devised a particular way of managing sheep or cattle and only bred from the females that really flourished under that system, within three or four generations I would have a flock or herd that did really well.

So if a red kite is a scavenger why isn't it built like a vulture? Why is it built like a tornado jet fighter? Because it's built for hunting. Six or seven years ago we would see a pair of red kites once a day as they toured the valley. When we were at the silage last week there were 18 sitting in a dead ash tree. It's a big success story for the species and I have no problem with that. But when is enough red kites enough? Plans have just been approved for a kite-feeding facility at a local visitor centre. It's not driven by love of kites, it's driven by a need to get more visitors. They have a problem making ends meet. It's a popular starting-off point for ramblers. They fill the car park with their cars, use the toilets and then set off without spending a penny (and if that isn't a contradiction I don't know what is!). So to get more visitors they are going to feed the kites. And what will be the repercussions?

The kites will flourish even more. I've got friends who live in the Chilterns. They reckon there are so many red kites there lots of other wildlife has suffered. So if the kites flourish even more than they are at present around here and they eat a lot of mice for example, what will happen to the owl population? It will decline. And who will get the blame for that? The farmers, of course, it's always the easy shot. So I finally ask the keeper what he thinks about the kite-feeding station. If I cull out the bad language there would just be a space between two full stops.

The people who are going to spend a fortune on grey partridge could learn a lot from gamekeepers. A few generations ago, keepers would pursue everything that wasn't game. The modern-day keeper is different. He knows how it all works in the countryside, he likes to see a balance and he knows how to achieve that balance. I just hope that in years to come the people who would change the countryside and its flora and fauna are held to account for the damage they have done.

★★★

There's been quite a lot on meadows on the TV recently. I think they look lovely, all those flowers, all those insects. But the reality is that by the time they are ready to cut, I've already cut my ryegrass twice. I can keep a cow on just over an acre of land, some to graze, some to cut for silage to keep the cow in the winter. If I had all meadows, I would struggle to keep a cow on three or four acres. So that means a third less cows, a third less milk a third less calves all against a background of a world population that has doubled in the last 40 years. All the meadows you see on TV are well populated with ragwort which is deadly poisonous if cut and fed to livestock. Naivety knows no bounds.

***

Is it just me? Am I the only one who can't get a new toothbrush out of its wrapper, not without a struggle anyway. The last one took me 15 minutes. The only advice I can give you is not to throw the old one in the bin before the new one is ready to use. I struggle with packaging. I was on a long journey last year and stopped on the motorway for a cup of coffee (and a pee); I wasn't really hungry but thought I'd have a packet of crisps to keep me going. I sat there for ages twisting and tearing at the packet to no avail. Then I remembered young people in the pub, nonchalantly clapping hands and it popping nicely open along the top. I tried this and it worked immediately. Except it wasn't the top of the bag that popped open, it was the bottom. The crisps went all over the floor. Finish the coffee and away, the tables weren't always that clean, goodness knows what the floor is like.

I'm into eating muesli and Greek yoghurt and honey at lunchtime. We had a new packet of muesli yesterday, a plastic packet. Couldn't open it. Last go, it ripped along the top and right down the side. Muesli everywhere. Scooped some into my dish, scooped some up and gave it the turkeys, but the floor is still a mess. Eat mine up quickly and leg it. I leave the kitchen door open, confidant that a passing hen will eat up the rest.

4 OCTOBER 2014

A quick bowl of cereal for lunch, no one about, mobile on silent, phone off the hook and I settle in my armchair for 20 minutes looking at the inside of my eyelids. About a minute into this power nap and there comes a determined knocking at the door. There's an urgency about it that demands response. It's a farmer from a couple of miles away who owns some fields that adjoin us. He's not a happy farmer and with good reason, he's just caught two dogs attacking his sheep. He's got one lamb in his Land Rover and it's badly ripped down its side. He's taking it to the vets and he's called by to ask me to keep a look out. He describes the dogs as a blue merle collie and a Labrador cross, they are not descriptions that I recognise. Thankfully (and it always crosses your mind), my dogs are all at the back door! At ten o'clock that evening a motorist calls to say our cows are on the road. I take a convenient grandson to investigate and they are our cows (I was hoping they were someone else's). Oddly they have forced the road gate open, the 'wrong' way. I put them in a neighbour's field for the night to get them off the road and out of harm's way. There is a plus in all this: they will get a free night's bed and breakfast. But I reflect as I drive home, there is something strange about it all.

We find out later the next day that another dairy herd a mile away but on the same road were also out that night and they too had pushed the gate open. The next night after that, another neighbour who lives close by is awakened by the sound of sheep bleating and dogs barking, off he goes in his pyjamas and wellies with his gun and torch and finds the same two dogs attacking the sheep. They pay him little attention, so absorbed are they in their frenzied attack, so with torch held close to barrel of gun in his left hand, he manages to shoot the blue dog. At the sound of the gun the other dog bolts away.

In the pub he's something of a hero: the consensus was that he's done well to shoot the dog and hold the torch at the same time. Two days later the Lab cross is at it again, killing two ewes, but this time it is shot as well. We think that it was almost certainly these two dogs that put our cows on the road and the other herd as well, we can't prove it but in the absence of any other explanation, it's all we've got.

When I was working on a farm when I left school we had dogs attacking our sheep. It was nearly 12 months before we could take our own dogs anywhere near the sheep, they would just panic. You can't imagine how much extra work that causes. But here's a strange thing. Both these dogs that have just been shot, looked well cared for. They looked as well cared-for as family pets can look. They were well fed, well groomed and had nice collars on, but no chips and no name discs. The police made extensive enquiries but to no avail. No one has been looking for these dogs or reported them missing. The consensus view is that they either belonged to some campers on holiday who had an inkling of what they'd been up to and didn't want to face the consequences or they had simply been dumped in the countryside. In either scenario we have a degree of irresponsibility that is breath-taking.

★★★

Call it a ritual, call it habit, call it what you like. I always do the same things in sequence when I get into the kitchen every morning. First and very important, put the kettle on for the first cup of tea (this is the one where I allow myself two sugars), which if you believe the newspapers, will probably kill me before the week is out. While the kettle boils I let the dogs in. This is very important as well. They will have heard me filling the kettle and they will be waiting by the door with their tails wagging. They know as well as I do that they can only come into the kitchen before 'anyone else' is about. If they stay too long they and I will get a serious bollocking. But that's changed a bit as well. I always leave the kitchen door open so that if we hear someone else coming they can make a bolt for it. And whilst the door is open a passing hen or two will enter as well. I think we've got about five hens and they live their lives as they choose and sometimes they choose to come into the kitchen. We've got a cockerel as well. He makes a lot of noise but he'll never make a Neville. Now I have noticed that there's always two or three hens waiting with the dogs to come in when I first get up.

I quite like hens in the kitchen, as they busy themselves about my feet. You can have a good conversation with a hen. Hens always know some gossip. The only downside thus far: these hens are not house-trained.

11 OCTOBER 2014

Bitter previous experiences tell me not to do this. It's a dangerous thing, for a farmer who does a bit of writing, to write about the weather. I think it's called tempting providence. But how can you not comment on the glorious weather we have had over the last few weeks? It's been a real pleasure to live and work in the countryside. All those lovely mornings, all the beauty of the autumn colours, I could go on and on almost endlessly. And I bet that wherever you live and whatever you do, you feel the same.

Stephen who works with us had what they call a 'working' day off one Sunday for his vintage tractor club: they wanted a piece of stubble to take their old tractors and ploughs, 'to put a shine on them'. I went up to see how they were getting on. They were on one of our top fields and when I got there most of the 'working' seemed to centre around sitting and drinking coffee and admiring the view. Soaking up the view would probably be a more accurate description. Some of them had been up there before, but not for many years, for some it was the first visit. And they just sat there, oozing contentment.

All that old equipment reminded me of when I used to drive it, but it was all nearly new then. Little tractors, little ploughs, but we managed. It put me in mind of when I was in agricultural college and we went on a farm visit. It was a terrible wet squally day, the heavy rain was relentless. It was on a large arable farm with a lot of sandy soil. We went into a 40-acre field that had been cleared of sugar beet and the field was being ploughed. It was being ploughed by three little tractors, a bit like the vintage ones in my field, each with a single furrow reversible plough on (I won't explain what a reversible plough is), each plough was turning over about 12 inches of ground at each pass and so the little procession of three tractors would only turn over a yard of ground every time they went down that huge field. There were no tractors cabs and the only weather protection the drivers had was a grain sack pinned over their shoulders with a nail and a sack over their knees. It was cold, it was very wet and the drivers were a picture of abject misery.

Of course some smart arse student has to ask the obvious question. 'Sir,' he says to the farmer, 'wouldn't it be more economic to have one larger tractor with a three furrow plough, then you would only have to employ one driver?' So the farmer agrees with him but goes on to explain that he needs three men in the spring to do all the sowing and hoeing, reaping and mowing, so a bit of very slow ploughing is giving the men something 'to do' during the quieter winter months.

Before mechanisation really kicked in, giving the men something 'to do' during the winter put farm workers into some horrible jobs. I've seen them working for days laboriously forking out strawed cattle yards by hand although there were tractors available to do the work in no time at all, then forking the muck out of trailers onto fields in orderly little heaps. Then weeks again spreading the muck by hand, acres and acres of it although there were plenty of machines that would do the work. All those miles of hedges trimmed by hand in the autumn, 'It's something they can do on a wet day'. Never mind how wet they get!

★★★

This autumn, there seem to be a lot of grey squirrels about. Perhaps it's been good weather for everything. But there also seem to be a lot of very young rabbits about, little tiny ones, as if the rabbit-breeding season has gone on a lot later than usual. Then there are the hares. There are still quite small leverets about. I always used to assume that hares bred only once, which was quite wrong. Someone said to me the other day that this year's hares appear to have had three or four hatches. Which is completely the wrong analogy but I think we all know what they meant.

★★★

Chat shows have guests. The guests always have an agenda. A book to sell or a film or play to promote. I don't for a minute try to put myself into that sort of category; to be honest, and I often am, I find that sort of self promotion a bit over the top. But not blatantly trying to go down the same route although it clearly looks as though I am, in order to tell you an anecdote, here goes. I've got this new book out and I get invited to do a 'signing' in a bookshop about 50 miles away. So I'm having a cup of tea with the nice lady who runs the shop and she says, 'I've not met you before, you do look so much like Ronnie Barker.' That completely threw me. I didn't know what to make of it. Still thinking about it two weeks later. Could be she has got confused, could be she meant George Clooney with a touch of Clint Eastwood (30 years ago)?

18 OCTOBER 2014

Because farmers generally get a hard time from the media and because they assume that the media speak on behalf of the general public, it is quite an easy thing for farmers to feel victimised. To see themselves as life's fall guys. I can understand how this happens, because despite your best efforts, there are sections of society that always see the worst in you.

I don't let it get to me because I don't really give a damn about what people think of me (perhaps you have already spotted this). I often feel that, if 'people' can't find a negative, they will make one up. It's as if they say to themselves, 'There's Roger Evans leaning on an oak tree, I bet he's got a chainsaw behind his back and he'll cut it down as soon as I'm out of sight.' Or, 'look at Roger Evans sitting in his truck watching those hares, he'll probably shoot them as soon as we are gone.'

I can give a more exact illustration of what I mean. There's a lot of hills around here, several go over the 1000ft mark, there's Iron Age Forts on two of them, what it must have been like down in the valley to make you want to live up there, goodness only knows. There's one hill, a big, high, long hill that is a particularly dominant feature of the area, and it has occurred to me several times recently that I've never been to the top of it, and I would like to.

At one time I could have run up it, not long ago I could have walked up it, now my knees need a ride up there and the views were just as spectacular as I'd imagined. We stopped for half an hour at the highest point and just took it all in. Seeing for miles and miles from a new perspective is always interesting. Where we are sitting is on the edge of a very steep side of the hill that drops down several hundred yards to the river. It's a large area, perhaps a couple of hundred acres, and it's covered with bracken and of very little use to man or beast. But the owner has planted hundreds of oak trees on it, I suppose they are 10 or 12ft high at the moment. I thought this was wonderful.

The next hill up the same river valley has a huge (it goes for a couple of miles) wood of deciduous trees that are such a riot of colour at this time of year that I always make a point of going out of my way just to have a look. In my mind's eye I could see this new plantation eventually emulating that wood further up the valley. What a spectacle it would be in 30 or so years' time: the one wood would complement the other, you can only imagine how wonderful it would be.

But not everyone sees it like that. Nestling at the foot of this hill is a lovely little village. A E Housman mentions it in a famous poem. Some people there have objected to the new oak trees. Their reason? When they eventually grow above the skyline they will increase the shade on the village and thus increase heating bills. Now I'm no tree expert but at a rough guess I would suspect that it will be 100-odd years before these particular trees get anywhere near the skyline. Do these people think they are going to live forever – they are all retired! It just beggars belief. It's as if they have nothing to do of any consequence in their own lives except look out of the window every day and look for something to complain about. No wonder famers think they are damned if they do and damned if they don't.

★★★

Whisper it quietly but, although I have been predicting the demise of the hedgehog for some time, mainly because hedgehogs come pretty high on the badger menu, I have seen more hedgehogs this year than I have seen for some time. OK so it's only four, but that's four more than I saw last year. One of my four was squashed on the road so I don't know if that counts but I didn't even see one squashed on the road last year. And anyway that's what hedgehogs do when there are lots of them, get squashed on the road, it's a sort of self-fulfilment. I know that four hedgehogs don't make a prickle, but it's a good step in the right direction. The proper collective noun for hedgehogs is an array, is four an array? I suspect they all need to be together to count as an array.

★★★

It's the vicar on the phone, wants to come round to see me. He's at the front door. Vicars always come to our front door. He tells me that he is preparing his sermon for Armistice Day and could I tell him any stories about what it was like to farm in the Second World War? It's Sunday afternoon, and he's a very nice vicar, politeness precludes me from suggesting he goes to Specsavers. But I do wonder how old he thinks I am and how old I actually look. I've still not recovered from being told that I look like Ronnie Barker. It's all testing my fortitude.

25 OCTOBER 2014

I've often said that when my daughter left home to get married, I missed three things. First and foremost and by some distance, I missed her. I'd always wanted a fair-haired daughter, I'd had one, and now she was leaving me. Secondly, I missed the money the wedding cost. We did most of it ourselves, we had a marquee on the lawn but we did all the food and drink, my wife made all the dresses. We tried to give her a £25,000 wedding for £10,000. I think we succeeded but you know how it works, 150 in the day and another 200 at night, and the trouble is the 150 that came in the day, don't go home. I said to her as we drove together to church, if you ever get married again it will be in the back room of the pub. And thirdly, I missed her presence in the bathroom. When I went to have a shower a whole range of treatments and lotions were available to me. I could wash my hair to put curls in it, next day I could wash it to straighten it. Next day I could put highlights in it or extra shine and body. The options were exciting and endless.

But time goes on. She's not far away and she's provided me with a fair-haired granddaughter, so I've been doubly blessed. My pocket money account is nearly replenished but I thought the bathroom experience was gone forever.

Then enter the scene two teenage grandsons. They frequently use my shower. Sometimes I can hardly get through the door for all the bottles of tack they leave in there. It's true they don't provide the range of options that a daughter used to provide, but I haven't bought shampoo for ages. There are multiple options of deodorants, which thus far I have avoided. I don't want to go to the pub smelling like a tart's boudoir (whatever that smells like!). Anyway, I'm not sure that they have the best taste. They've got their hair cut like those characters on the TV programme, *Peaky Blinders*, and why would you want your hair cut like that?

★★★

Down the backyard to the house comes the man who reads the electricity meter. He strides along with confidence. He has a stout hazel thumbstick in his hand. The dogs all bark at him but they keep their distance, wary of the stick. But the stick is not a precaution against dogs. After he has read the meter in the kitchen he has to go into the old walled garden where the meter for the milking parlour is. In the old walled garden is where the turkeys live. The stick is protection against aggressive turkey stags. He tells me that he is the only meter reader at his depot that has to carry a stick. He says that the turkeys are more of a hazard than any of the dogs he meets. He takes it all in good spirits. He's photographed my turkeys with his phone and shown the photos to his colleagues. They all think he's a hero. It makes me quite proud, to think the fame of my turkeys has spread far and wide.

★★★

There's new tenants in our pub. Not a lot of changes have they brought with them, but one thing that has changed is the beer. So the regulars have been trying the different beers as they search for one that suits them. But the search is based mainly on flavour, they read the names of the beers, but they pay little regard to the alcohol percentage. It's an interesting phenomenon, some people have settled on a beer they like, completely unaware that they have become more talkative. Applied to someone who previously had little to say, this can be quite amusing. But when it is applied to someone who had little to say because they actually *had* little to say, it can be a long evening. Far better when they were quiet. Other people are affected in a different way. Some people fall over as they make their way home through the village. Some people leave holes in the hedges.

1 NOVEMBER 2014

Many years ago the country was overrun with rabbits. A feature of all fields, whether they carried cereal crops, roots, or just grass, was the 20 yards or so that was grazed bare around every field by rabbits. My wife's father, who probably employed seven men full time after the war, would put two of them to catch rabbits as soon as harvest was finished in the autumn until it was spring again and they would be diverted to work the load that came with it. They'd probably be pulled away from rabbit-catching to help to thresh the stacks of corn but for nearly six months they would catch rabbits. That's most days they would go with ferrets and nets to catch rabbits because there were so many of them. They would be sold regularly to a dealer and there would be so many of them they would find their way into towns and in the war years they were an important source of protein for the whole nation. That is not to forget their importance to the farm. They might devastate crops but the cumulative effect of the two men catching rabbits would be enough to pay the rent on my father-in-law's farm. All that finished with myxomatosis. I see rabbits every day now. It crossed my mind the other day that they were getting quite plentiful again. The day after that I saw a myxomatosis-affected rabbit sitting in the middle of the road in all its misery. And that seems to be how it is these days: rabbit numbers fluctuate but as soon as they seem to get plentiful, along comes a fresh outbreak of the disease.

★★★

Why are people quite content for the world to see spectacles perched on the end of their nose yet if they need help with their hearing they want to keep that aid out of sight? I don't need a hearing aid, well, not yet anyway, but I have developed a very selective form of hearing. My wife can talk to me in the evening about some family matter and then ask my opinion and I haven't heard a word she has said. I've got a friend who has struggled with his hearing for years and it's become something of a joke. When he's in the pub and someone is telling a story, as soon as the story is finished out he comes with 'What's he say?' But if someone asks him, quite quietly, if he wants another drink, he always hears that.

His hearing, or lack of it, was becoming an issue for his family because he always had the television on so loud, they couldn't bear it. When he was watching *Coronation Street* they would stand in the garden and lean in through the window to watch it. Eventually he agreed to have a hearing aid. He put it in when he came home from work one night, had his tea and it worked really well. So his wife said, 'You go and watch the news and I'll bring you another cup of tea'. Which she did and then the phone went and almost frightened the life out of him and he spilled the scalding cup of tea in his 'lap'. He's not used the aid since.

★★★

They are quite big on medical advice at the pub. Everyone has a pet remedy for common ailments. Most are best avoided at all costs. I remember one young lad having a particular chesty cough and they persuaded him that the best cure was to rub Vick onto the soles of his feet, when he went to bed, which he did diligently for a week. He was really pleased that the cough went after a week and thought the process had worked. Never crossed his mind that the cough might have gone after a week anyway. I'm just as gullible. They told me to spray my knees with WD40 (used to free rusty bolts), to take the stiffness out of them. And I tried it!

8 NOVEMBER 2014

We've got a room we all call the office. It's true there's a desk in there and a phone. But it's quite difficult to see either because the office is full of children's toys and junk that should mostly have been thrown away years ago. But there's some shrubs and bushes outside the window and there are always wrens to be seen there. So this winter I am going to help the wrens. I'm going to feed them in cold weather and I'm going to put a box for them to huddle in when it's cold. I like to see them. I'm going to give wrens a helping hand.

★★★

Two sad tales. When Mert first arrived here, he liked to chase vehicles. It was a habit he had brought with him as a sort of legacy from the farm where he was born, where the ten or so dogs there are much given to a bit of vehicle chasing. We weren't much bothered about his habit at first, it was after all a part of his fierce dog image: 'I'll bite you when you come here and I'll chase you off the yard when you go.' If the vehicle was going slow enough, he would indulge in a bit of tyre biting as well. He was quite good at tyre biting and would puncture the tyres on the post van on quite a regular basis. The postman took all this changing of wheels in amazingly good spirits, far better than I would have done myself.

But Mert went a bit over the top one week, three punctures, and we had a letter from the sorting office to say that in future we would have to pay for new tyres. So we stopped him at that, and he'd been castrated and was less aggressive, and getting older, so the tyre biting died out.

Then we got a young sheepdog bitch and she starts it all over again. The corgi thinks it's a wonderful game and joins in with great enthusiasm. The frenzied barking that went on when someone got in their car rouses Mert from his slumbers and he remembers the days of his misspent youth and joins in as well. So there are now three dogs going berserk, chasing vehicles. I was most worried about Mert because as he was still targeting the tyres and getting old and less sprightly, he was the most likely to get run over.

They didn't chase me because I would bellow at them. But when someone else got in their car, the dogs would go into such a frenzy while seat belts were being put on that fights would break out. It was mostly the corgi that would start the fights and then she would retreat under the car where the other dogs couldn't get at her. It was only a matter of time before the inevitable happened and the corgi went under a wheel and had to be put down.

We've had corgis here for fifty years and it seems strange to be without one. I suspect we won't be without one for long, I'm looking to see if I can find one at a dog rescue centre, it seems like a nice thing to do. Have you seen how much corgi puppies are? To put it into perspective, the cheapest one I have seen would cost me the equivalent of 2,400 litres of milk! Which is an unfortunate but real way of showing how much buying power a litre of milk gives you! And that would be for a puppy without any papers. Still, I have never had any papers and I seem to have managed.

Far less sad, but a bereavement of sorts, nonetheless, is the departure of my Jag. I'd had it well over three years now, I bought it very cheaply when my grandson and I took a bit of a flyer on eBay and it's been, by far, the best car I've ever had. But my own life has moved on, I no longer have to do much long distance driving on business, I now need something that I can turn off a lane and drive over a field. So exit the ten-year-old Jag and enter a seven-year-old four-wheel drive. Not that I am superstitious but I thought it would be a bit of a long shot to find two good vehicles in succession on eBay, so I bought the 4x4 in the more conventional way by part exchange.

So the man says 'I'll bring the 4x4 across at 12.30.' And I say that's fine because I've got to go off to a rugby match at 2pm. So he turns up at 2.45! And I'm getting a bit tetchy. For a start I can't cope with being late, it's about the only thing that winds me up. And it's a Friday afternoon. If you ever hear travel bulletins on Friday afternoon, they go on forever. And this is the Friday afternoon that precedes school half term, and I've got a hundred miles to go. So I'm a bit terse with him, pay him and get in the vehicle and drive off. No time for a look around.

After about five miles my bad mood evaporates and I allow myself to take it all in. It's too hot in here, how do you control that? How do you wash the windscreen, stuff like that. Then I notice quite a large 'S' in the middle of the digital display. Wonder what that means? It's got an automatic gearbox so perhaps I am in sports mode. But if I'm in sports mode it will be using more diesel than

I need to use, wonder how I alter that? (Anyway I haven't been sporty for a long time.)

After about 30 miles I come to my first set of traffic lights (that's how it is around here), and whilst I'm on red I play around with the gear levers but the 'S' still persists. Then ten miles further on the 'S' turns to an 'E'. That's better, I must have done something, I'm in 'economical' now, that's much better. But it's only better for a short while because the 'E' turns into an 'N'! Try as I may, I can't think of anything that is relevant to my motoring that begins with 'N'. I know that neutral begins with 'N', but if I was in neutral I wouldn't be making progress. This progression from 'S' to 'E' and then 'N' has completely baffled me, the car is going OK so I'm hoping it's not serious. Then I go around a corner and the 'N' changes to 'NW'. Got it! It's a bloody compass. Why would I need a compass, never needed one before? What does it think I am, some sort of matelot?

15 NOVEMBER 2014

I'm always a bit sheepish about admitting that we take the *Daily Mail*. I often try to justify its contents, by saying that it's Ann's paper and that I sometimes read it. But reading it on Sunday quite made my day. I refer to the article about a letter by Sir Ian Botham criticising the RSPB. About time someone did. I don't bother to examine their finances but when he says that 'it has betrayed bird lovers and the species it is meant to save', he is spot on. I have been banging on endlessly for years about some of the predator species getting completely out of hand, to the detriment of so much of the wildlife (and bird life) we love. 'You forgot the birds' is a very appropriate name for his campaign. The RSPB are trying to link the problems to shooting interests. Large-scale commercial shooting, like fox hunting, is difficult to justify, other than to say you enjoy it.

But if you get a really prolonged cold spell in the winter, where are all the small birds to be found? In the pheasant woods helping themselves to all the wheat on offer. The RSPB are wealthy and powerful. And we all know what happens to that sort of combination. Make no mistake, the RSPB has more influence on what goes on in the British countryside than any other organisation. The Department for Environment, Food and Rural Affairs (DEFRA) and Natural England run scared of the RSPB. In fact if there is any running going on, it is the RSPB that are 'running' those two bodies. I used to despair of their power and influence, but the mighty can fall: look what's happened to Tesco.

★★★

Yesterday there was a jay on our lawn, today there were two. I can't remember the last time I saw a jay on this farm, it's got to be years and years. Now jays are reputed to do as much damage to eggs and fledglings as magpies but there's an important point here. Jays are not as plentiful as magpies therefore, collectively, they don't do as much damage. So these jays can happily set up camp here for the time being, it's all about balance, as usual. More bird news. Over the other side of the road, on a field of my neighbour's, 18 lapwings have been there for a week now. It's good to see them there, so good to see their swirling flights. It's a good field for them to breed on. Plenty of places for their chicks to drink. Just a pity there are so many predators about.

★★★

Most people in the pub have finished drilling their winter corn. As always, when people bring their stories to the pub there is a competitive element to it all. Because of how the fields 'roll' around here, you can always see a lot of what your neighbours are doing. 'How big was that field you were ploughing today?' 'Forty five acres.' 'I bet it was.' 'It was.' 'What speed were you ploughing at?' 'Six miles an hour.' It's been like that for a few weeks now: who can plough the most acres a day, whose tractor will plough the fastest. Then just the same discussion on drilling. It's the same all the year round as the farming activities follow the calendar. But there's been a new element this autumn. Seagulls. Seagulls following the plough are a time-honoured tradition. We've always had a few around here, but only a few, we are after all, a long way from the seaside. This year there have been lots and lots. 'There were 50 seagulls following my plough today.' 'I had 100.' How they count them when they are flying beats me, they can't find room to land because of all the kites and buzzards. I've never trusted seagulls ever since one had my ice cream as I came off the pier at Llandudno. I think that most seagulls are fifth columnists. I'm not sure what that means, but it seems to describe them.

22 NOVEMBER 2014

Spring, summer, autumn, winter. The four seasons progress seamlessly one to the other. The impression is that there are three months of each. But for farmers it's not quite like that. In the autumn the more dry weather we can get the better, the more dry weather we have, the longer we can keep the cattle out in the fields. The longer they are outside, the later the onset of the winter workload. But three or four wet days can change all that. On a farm, winter can come in a week.

★★★

I suppose most of us, if we have a longish journey to make, put some sort of thought into it. If I have to go a long way and if I am careful what I consume before I set out, I can usually drive for three hours before I take a break. The three hours is not dictated by the onset of fatigue but the need to have a pee! That is why I have to give some thought to what I consume before I set out. But if it's a 4-hour journey, a break after two hours seems fairly logical. So you go into services and do the necessary and go for a cup of tea or coffee. And 'they' say, 'small, medium or large?' And you say 'small', you still have two hours to go, remember. And they bring you the small cup that is just about as big as a bucket, the only difference is that a bucket had a handle on the top and this has a handle on the side. I know you don't have to drink it all, but what a waste.

★★★

Much as I love my turkeys, they are getting out of hand. I've got three stags and two hens. My idea was to have a nice little flock of turkeys that lived about the yard, free to come and go as they pleased. They look nice, a small flock, people don't expect to see them, so generally they think that they are nice as well. It's always worked OK in the past. But free range, come and go as you please, turkeys are vulnerable to the fox so every now and again you have to buy some more. And that's always worked in the past as well. Two or three hen turkeys scratching and foraging about the yard with a resplendent stag watching over them, putting his feather display on, going red and blue about his head and neck, as if to burst (heart attack imminent?) and seeking out anything reflective to challenge his own image to a fight. Clean cars were very suitable for this purpose, never a problem for my car, and low windows and the like.

We once had a stag turkey that fell in love with a bucket and he would spend hours displaying to the bucket. I don't think the love was ever consummated, but it wasn't for the want of trying. But what to do with the turkeys I have now? The stags are so aggressive. It's almost worse than when Neville the cockerel was at the height of his powers. People phone me to see if it is OK to call! People walk long diversions to avoid walking through our yard. Children are not safe. So something had to be done. There are two very big aggressive stags and a smaller, less aggressive stag. So I start to wonder if I could put the two big ones somewhere where they wouldn't be a problem and let the two hens and the little stag out to see how he behaved. Then I thought about the keeper's pheasant release pens. He's got one very big pen with a high fence all around it, plenty of wheat in there, a stream and a pond. A veritable turkey paradise! So I asked the keeper the big question and he agreed immediately. Keepers are usually very amenable at this time of year. It's the start of their shooting season and it's important to keep everyone on-side. Besides it's no big deal, there are already four cockerels in there anyway. Two were mine and two he bought himself. He reckons they keep the pheasants together, so two turkeys might be even better.

That night Stephen and I go to catch the two big stags. This was a mistake. One black turkey, in the dark, looks very much like any other black turkey. So we didn't catch the two biggest. I was to find this out to my cost the next morning when I went, nonchalantly, to feed the remaining three. I went stickless, thinking the two nasty ones had gone. That was a big mistake. I had a really scary fight with the biggest of the three: the only defence I had was a swinging bucket. So I still can't let the turkeys out because the worst one is still here at home! But what of the other two? The morning after we put them out in the pheasant pen, I'm going around the cattle and I meet the keeper on his pheasant-feeding rounds. He tells me that the turkeys have expelled the cockerels from the pen and the cockerels are now in a wood half a mile away. 'What are the turkeys doing today?' 'Last time I saw them, they were chasing squirrels.'

29 November 2014

When my son was single he would go off to play rugby mid morning on Saturdays and usually return while I was having my breakfast on Sunday. I'm not sure why it took him so long, the rugby club is only 14 miles away. Anyway he'd join me at breakfast and give me a report on yesterday's match and where he'd gone during the evening, which was usually more interesting than the game of rugby. 'When I was driving home this morning,' he tells me, 'I saw a camel looking over a gate.' 'I bet you did.' And I give him a mild lecture on his drinking habits. Next Saturday afternoon

I go to watch him play rugby and there in the lane just where he told me, looking over the same gate, is a camel. Seems a local travelling circus is wintering at a nearby farm. Seems like we have a problem with camels in our family.

★★★

It's getting to the time of year when you get to the end of your diary. Stuff that's due to happen in a few months' time can be found on the back page. I've not got a lot down for next year, it doesn't do to plan too far ahead at my age. But I do have a date in February when I have to go to the village hall one night to talk to the WI. The date has been written down for some time but now it's getting nearer, it's getting a bit scary. Not something to underestimate, your Women's Institute. You assume that it's all about Jerusalem and making jam, at your peril. They've visibly shaken prime ministers, have the WI. You need to be on your mettle.

Just to endorse my concerns, a story comes in of a WI meeting a few villages away. They are being given a talk by a member of a local wildlife trust about the flora and fauna that can be found in their area. The talk is very ably illustrated by a film just to show what animal and bird life can be found right under your noses. So the camera is taking them around familiar woods, fields and lanes when a lady calls out 'Can you stop the film and go back a bit?' 'Of course I can,' says the man, pleased that he has members of his audience so clearly concentrating on what he is showing. He reverses the film, video, DVD, whatever it is, until a voice calls out, 'Stop it there.' Which he does.

Heads are turned one to the other and whispered conversations are taking place, messages are passed backwards and forwards from row to row until the whispering is stilled and all the ladies are sitting quietly again and he is told to proceed. He is really perplexed by this. The shot that had caught one of the ladies attention, and clearly fascinated all the other ladies, was a fairly simple shot of two red kites soaring over a small valley.

So he finished his presentation, answered some questions, had his tea and cake, and the ladies, chattering quite animatedly, started to disperse. The chairperson is hovering quite near, to see him away and to offer any help should it be needed, so when she is the last lady in the room he returns to the still in his film that had caused all the interest. He tells her that particular shot had never created a reaction like that anywhere else. 'What,' he asks, 'was so special about those two kites?' 'Well,' says the lady, drawing a bit closer and lowering her voice, with a bit of a shifty look around her to make sure everyone else is gone, 'in the shot, at the bottom of the valley is a lane that runs within the fields. And parked on one side of the lane, on the grass, under a tree, was the 4x4 of a farmer who lives just outside the village and the nice Audi convertible of a lady who moved here 12 months ago, whose husband is away in London all week.' Keen-eyed, your WI members, don't miss much. A true story. Could be a sad story or an unlucky story, depends on your point of view.

6 December 2014

The corn is all safely in the shed. Next year's seed corn is all safely in the ground (and growing nicely thank you). The harvest festivals have been and gone, traditional hymns sung and thanks been given. Probably the biggest thank you this year should have been reserved for the dry weather. Most corn was harvested in dry conditions which was a godsend because prices have fallen unbelievably and the last thing we wanted was a wet harvest and huge drying bills to pay. Anyway, I digress, harvest is done and dusted, finished, for yet another year.

But it isn't, is it? In some ways it never is. Lots of farms grow maize now for livestock feed and the maize harvest is usually later than the traditional church services. We don't grow maize any more but we're not finished either. We've got ten acres of fodder beet to harvest. This is done in November. When it's cold. The field in question is up on top land, where it's always cold.

Stephen is carting trailer loads back to the yard and I'm waiting with the loader to pile it up into a big heap. There's a really cold wind blowing and one of our machines is minus a cab door. No prizes for guessing which one I'm on! When it's 'bait' time I drive up to the field to have a sandwich with Stephen and the contractor who is doing the lifting. Don't usually say this but it's a good crop of beet we are lifting. My agronomist (that's someone who takes his dogs for a walk around your fields) reckons it's the best crop of beet he's seen for years. Sadly, no one can admire it from the road, which is yet another of the ironies of farming life. If it was by the road, it would probably be a very poor crop. That's how farming life usually works. It's a good crop because it had plenty of poultry manure, my farming equivalent of a gro-bag. Cheap chicken is not the only good thing to come out of intensive chicken sheds!

The leaves of the beet are about knee-high and form a sort of dense canopy that hides lots of pheasants. As the machine trundles up and down the field removing two rows at a time, it destroys all the sanctuaries where the cock pheasants have their territories. They only spend their days there, they go off to roost as it gets dark, but that doesn't mean that they can't have a good fight in the meantime.

Fodder beet is a wonderful animal feed, it is so palatable that my cows will fight over it. You can feed it whole, you can chop it up and mix it with other feeds. You can feed it down a trough in a shed or scatter it out on fields for sheep or cattle. Or you can leave it where it is, in the fields, in its rows, and graze it off with sheep or cattle. We have left five acres in the fields besides the ten we've lifted, for just this purpose. If you've got too much, you can always sell some.

Now here's the thing. Anything you can feed to livestock you can feed to a digester and turn it into power. There are digesters being installed everywhere. Digesters love fodder beet as much as livestock does. I've been saying this for years but no one seems to listen. It starts to get scary. Inflation is quite low, which we are told is a good thing. Inflation is low, in part, because food is worth less. So if you had the option of feeding grass, corn, maize, straw or fodder beet to an animal but you could make more money out of it to produce power, which would you do? It's quite a simple option. If power is more expensive than food, what then? Think about it. Could be more power and less food. Could be cheap food is not the win-win politicians think it is.

★★★

I went to speak at a Young Farmers' dinner last Friday. I thought it was in Gloucestershire but when I came home next day, the sign on the motorway said I was entering, not leaving, Gloucestershire, so I'm not really sure where I was. It was at a very posh venue and I had to wear evening dress. I never like wearing what they call 'black tie'. When you spill food down your shirt, which I usually do, everyone can see it, and you haven't got a conventional tie to try to hide it. My wife reckons that looking down the front of my clothes is like reading a menu. And she is right, in fact at the dinner in question I chose my food specifically to avoid spillage, gravy to be avoided at all costs.

I was invited to a posh dinner in London years ago. A week after I accepted the invitation, the girl who invited me phoned up to tell me it was a black tie occasion. I said 'OK'. An hour later she phoned to ask 'You do know what black tie means, do you?' I said 'Of course I do, it's what you wear to funerals.' I've just been out to my car to have a look to see where I'd been. It was South Beaufort Young Farmers and the venue was Courtworth Court, very posh. It was their 70th anniversary dinner and several people came up and said nice things about what I write for my column on Saturdays. Anyway this very attractive lady in a red dress comes up and I think she's going to ask me for a dance. This could have presented a problem, I've got bad arthritis in one knee and the other is a lot worse, then there's the walking stick to contend with. But no need to worry, she's come to tell me that when she had her operation (details to follow next week) she had been banned from reading my articles in case she laughed too much and burst her stitches. Assuming that was a compliment, it was an unusual one.

13 December 2014

A tale of two piggys. I'd like to have a pig. A sow pig. One that would have piglets that might run around the yard. The sort of pig that would become a good friend. Strangely, everyone in the family agrees with me. Strange because apart from me, the two people who mention it (the pig) the most are my two eldest grandsons who don't see careers for themselves in farming. The only barrier to the piggy presence is somewhere suitable to keep it. Because we don't have anywhere, we'd have to build somewhere. Not least amongst our needs would be a concrete pad so that the pig couldn't dig its way to freedom. Concrete and pig houses would cost money, something we don't have to spare and are unlikely to have for over 12 months. The demise of profitability in dairy farming is really starting to have an effect. Things are tight, really tight. I can't see there being any improvement until at least next autumn. Twelve months ago the Chinese were busy buying dairy products and creating a buoyant trade. A trade they have pulled out of. The Russians have stopped buying EU cheese: they used to buy 250,000 tons a year. Obviously they didn't buy all that from the UK, but that big tonnage of cheese is still out there looking for a home and helping to undermine the market.

That's the problem with dairy production. It's not like making nuts and bolts. If there are too many nuts and bolts about, you go onto a 3-day week or switch the factory off for a couple of weeks at Christmas. The only way you can cut off dairy production to the sort of extent that will make any difference, is to kill a lot of cows. That's not what we are about so that's not an option, but that's the reality of it. Quite why dairy farmers should have a hard time because of what goes on in the Ukraine eludes me, but that's how it is. Enough of this whinging, none of us have to be dairy farmers, no one owes us a living, but if we shut up shop, and 400 have done that already this year alone, where will all the milk, cheese, cream etc come from?

I have a friend who has the perfect pig. She has only the one, for exactly the same reasons that I want one. But she has an old traditional range of brick-built buildings where the pig lives. The pig lives in a nice loose box. Nothing unusual about that, except that the door is always open, night and day, it's wide open. The pig lies down to sleep all night in the straw and stands in the doorway all day with its head sticking out. It's where the people on the farm walk by frequently and she gets a pat on the head from everyone who passes by. They've tried in vain to get her out onto the yard but she refuses to budge through the doorway. When she has piglets, the little pigs run out on the yard but she refuses to follow.

When I last kept a solitary sow, one of the biggest problems was getting her to a boar. You had to have a licence to get them there and another to get them back. If the sow didn't conceive, you had the same process to go through again. There's just about as much freedom of movement for pigs as there would be if you turned up at Heathrow dressed in black with a Kalashnikov under your arm, seeking to board a flight for Turkey. None of that hassle for my friend, she uses artificial insemination, successfully, and does the job herself!

★★★

Pig story two. Another friend of mine thought he'd like to have a pig, once again for the same reasons. Anyway he locates an in-pig gilt of the sort he would like, about a hundred miles away. So he goes to see her, likes her, and pays for her. He says he will return to collect her with his trailer. You should never take a trailer with you when you go to buy livestock, it makes you look too keen! But he doesn't rush to fetch the gilt. He decides to leave it as long as possible. He is quite taken with the idea that it's his pig, he's paid for it, but the vendor is still having to feed it.

Then the phone calls start, 'This gilt is getting close to farrowing, you need to fetch her.' He leaves it a couple more days then he sets off, truck and trailer and wife, to fetch it. When he gets there the vendor is flapping, he thinks she'll farrow at any time. They put plenty of nice straw in the trailer, load the gilt and off they go. They stop after ten miles to see if the gilt is OK and find she's already had one piglet. My friend says he will get into the trailer to keep an eye on things and his wife will drive gently home. The big problem with farrowing is that the sow will have one pig, get up to have a look at it, then as she flops down to have the next, she will crush the one she's just had. That's why my friend is getting into the trailer.

So his wife drives carefully home and when she gets there she gets out of the truck as quietly as she can, she tiptoes back to the trailer and peeps inside. The gilt is lying comfortably down the length of the trailer. She has eight lovely piglets suckling away at her teats, a picture, mother and piglets, of contentment. Also contented is her husband, my friend, he's lying flat out on the straw on the other side, propped comfortably against the gilt's back, fast asleep.

20 December 2014

There's an item on the news today about trying to reduce the number of so-called nuisance phone calls. We get one at one o'clock every lunchtime from the same company. It's at about the time of day, that if I can, I close my eyes for ten minutes. I try to remember to take the phone off the hook, but if I do, I don't always remember to put it back on again! Yesterday I had a phone call and a machine said that they wanted to speak to me about the accident I had just had but that all their operators were busy and would I hang on until one was free? So in theory that was a nuisance phone call about a nuisance phone call. What's all that about?

★★★

I don't yet seem to have donned my yuletide cloak of grumpiness. My friends and family are circling me warily. They know that it is all matter of time, they know from bitter experience that it's all a matter of time. Truth is, I've been a bit distracted, I've been distracted by corgi pups and falling milk prices. And the two are linked, as we shall see. I had it in mind to buy a new corgi pup in time for Christmas. Cheer everyone up, I thought. Especially me, who doesn't like being corgi-less. So, as corgi pups are getting scarce, I look for one on my laptop. Just out of interest, and as a digression, several other breeds are getting scarce. Boxers, Rottweilers, Dobermans are in decline. Why is that? Tails are why. Corgis, like the other three breeds I have just mentioned, look, in the opinion of the people who might buy them, naff. The opinion is that long tails don't suit them, so they don't buy one. The irony is that the people who have clamoured for an end to tail-docking of puppies have had their way, but at what cost? And what have they achieved? They've saved the tail but they are losing the dog. Smart, isn't it?

Anyway, back to my laptop. Corgi puppies for sale, there's a few about £600 with no papers, up to £750. So we will focus on the £600, no papers. Not a big issue. I've never had papers and have struggled through. But at the back of my mind in all I do at present, are milk prices. You will have picked up, via the media, that on-farm milk prices are less than the cost of production, but on-farm milk prices vary from farm to farm. But there is a reality to it, the reality is not just how much you get per litre, it's to do with how much that litre of milk will buy in the outside world, how far will it go towards buying your inputs? So I've started valuing things in litres of milk, and it's not a nice scenario. At the pub, a pint of beer costs £3. I don't drink pints because of driving, but I buy them for the people I drink with. Rounding things up a bit, but not much, I have to sell 4½ litres of milk to get a £1. And 4½ litres of milk is a gallon. So a pint of beer cost three gallons of milk. Why would I want to swap three gallons of milk for one pint of beer? I wouldn't and I won't. So I've started staying home a bit more. But it gets worse. Using the same formula, a corgi pup without papers will cost you 600 gallons of milk. That's 60 churns in old money. Now we can manage without a new corgi, but if something breaks, and it often does, you don't get much in the way of repairs or spare parts for £600. That's the reality, that's the sort of recessionary pressure on dairy farmers.

★★★

I'm used to being cold and wet outside. It's a given, for a farmer. But I don't like being cold and wet when I'm in the house, which can also be a given in this house. Years and years ago we put in central heating, we put it in for our B&B guests' benefit. So it's quite easy to have our house very warm. But there is no insulation and no double-glazing, and heating is very expensive. So there's always this dilemma, if there's no guests in, how much can you afford to turn it all on? Not much, to be honest. The problem is my wife has discovered how to switch it on, so I seem to spend most of my time switching it off. Sometimes she has the house so hot it melts the frost on the lawn. But the real prize goes to B&B guests who come in late after we've gone to bed and leave the front door open all night.

27 December 2014

I used to have a few different roles within the dairy industry. For a farmer it was life-changing stuff. Here, there and everywhere, miles upon miles in the car, hotels, trains and planes. Sounds idyllic but much of it was overrated. The mile upon mile in the car might very well be spent nose-to-tail on a motorway, in terrible weather, where to lose your concentration for a second could have dire consequences. You could take an early train to London which might mean a four o'clock start from home. The ticket might have cost a fortune but you might still have to stand all the way there. And just to rub it in, you might have to stand all the way back as well. Plane travel is overrated also. But I don't regret a bit of it, because what bit I might have contributed was done for fellow dairy farmers, so that made it all worthwhile. Of course there were lots and lots of bonuses, out and about, often in the countryside, meeting lots of very nice people. I actually miss it a bit. But life moves on and you have to move on with it.

If I had to pick out a memorable day amid that sort of life, one that always springs to mind is the Ceremony of the Christmas Cheeses at the Royal Hospital Chelsea. This is organised by what we call The Dairy Council, an organisation that dairy farmers should be proud of. Probably its main role is the work it does on food nutrition, working with health professionals promoting the consumption of dairy products as part of a balanced diet, especially for young girls, and the bit of its work I particularly like is what it does to counter alarmist anti-dairy stories from organisations that might have another agenda altogether.

Vegans will plant anti-dairy stories, for example, but it's not just that they are anti-milk, they are anti-cow as well. They don't want milk because they don't want farm animals.

Anyway, every year the Dairy Council present a huge table of different cheeses to the Chelsea pensioners at a ceremony at the Royal Hospital. Cheese is donated by almost every cheese manufacturer in the country, large and small, and it is quite a sight when it is all accumulated together on the large table. You assemble for coffee and are hosted by army officers in their dress uniforms, plumed hats as well. When all guests are present, you are led to the Great Hall where the ceremony takes place. It's a magnificent hall and about 40-50 of the pensioners, resplendent in their red coats, are already present. There is an army string section in one corner playing background music and we, the guests, sit down in rows facing the cheese table.

When the main party enter the room, they do so to a fanfare of trumpets played by soldiers – this year I think from the Welsh Guards. The cheeses are blessed by the padre and there are a couple of speeches. When the formalities are finished, there are drinks and canapés and a chance to mingle with the pensioners. We always finish up with singing 'The Quartermaster's Stores', which is presumably where the cheese ends up. Then it's off to the magnificent state apartments for lunch. What a nice day out. And the nice thing is I still get invited, it might be computer error, but it is still nice.

Anyway, the thing is, if you are mixing with army officers in dress uniform, well it's a suit job isn't it? No need to put dress code on the invites, it's clearly 'dress tidy'. But it's December, you need more than your suit, don't you, it's probably going to be cold.

If you go to a rural funeral in the winter in a small country church, chances are that, if you are not family, you could be standing outside. I've done that, shivering, lots of times. And as I've shivered, I've envied those fellow farmers clad in huge warm overcoats. So I determined to have one as well. I've got a good friend who works in a charity shop and over the course of six months she found us three at £15 each. So now the family all have nice warm overcoats. So it's the overcoat that I throw into the back seat of the car.

It's dark when I get to the station, it's dry and it's very cold. I open the back door of the car to get the overcoat out and see there is also another coat there as well. The posh overcoat weighs a ton, could be more, do I need to be carrying that about all day? No I don't, that other coat is one of several that dairy farmers are given by companies. They carry motifs but they keep out the wet and cold. So I opt for the shorter lighter one.

When I get to the platform and under the lights I soon find that I have committed myself to going to a posh do in London, where I will mix with army officers in dress uniform, the great and the good of the UK dairy industry, and I will be wearing the old working coat I wear around the farm that is literally covered with the stuff that comes out of cows when they lift their tails up.

3 JANUARY 2015

Much as I love my dog Mert, it has never crossed my mind to take him to the pub. Why ever would I want to take him to the pub? I don't go to the pub for the drink, I go for the company. So what would be the point of sitting in the pub with the landlady, just the two of us, and she saying to me, 'It's quiet in here tonight,' and lying on the floor near the door, would be Mert, a black bundle of growls. If I took him on a regular basis, people would know and stay away. He's really starting to show his age now but lots of people still arrive on the yard and phone me on their mobiles and ask me to come and escort them to the house. This is all good stuff. It gives Mert a reputation. He's a bit like an aging gunslinger in the Westerns I watch. They all know he's getting past it but they are not taking any chances. (Lots of people who come here still keep a wary eye out for Neville the cockerel and he's been gone two years now.)

I was just going to write down that I would be just as likely to take Mert to the pub as I would a turkey stag, but that wouldn't be true, because taking a turkey stag to the pub has crossed my mind several times. I'd take him to the pub when it was busy and be confident that there would be five minutes of chaos. After five minutes I would be barred from taking a turkey there again. But I might be barred myself and I daren't take a chance on that.

I meant to be writing about dogs in pubs. Lots of people do take their dogs to the pub. Some dogs sit down quietly and are as good as gold. Some dogs are a total pain in the arse. It came as no surprise to me, and probably no surprise to you either, when I report that in categorising the dogs, their owners fall into identical categories. Some owners even take dogs in there on those retracting leads, so that they might be sitting there chatting and the dog is two rooms away being a nuisance trying to eat people's crisps, whilst sneaking through the pub at about shin-height is this dog lead tripping people up.

We've recently had two new additions to the doggy contingent. Two regulars have acquired spaniel pups. All pups of all breeds are cute, but there is something very special about a spaniel pup. So if the pups are put onto the floor, as they often are, everyone is making puppy type noises, trying to make a fuss of them. Everyone, that is, except me. I sit there and ignore them with an affected nonchalance. It's not that I don't like them, but I don't inflict my dogs on other people in the pub and I don't really want them inflicting their dogs on me.

But there's a strange thing. Everyone is trying to attract these spaniels to them, but the pups ignore them and head straight for me. So it ends up, that the only thing getting a fuss made of it, is me. This hasn't gone unnoticed. There have been jealous glances made. I had assumed that I was attractive to the pups because I emanated some sort of doggy charisma. That's not what anybody else thinks. Someone who regularly attracts the attentions of spaniels? They all think I'm dealing drugs.

★★★

You have to go down about six or seven steps in the pub to go from the bar to the loos. That's not to say that they are in the cellar, it's just that they are on a different level. Last week there was a pipe leaking in the ceiling at the top of the stairs so there was a large bucket placed there to catch the drips (with suitable warning signs). So I suggested to the landlady that as the bucket was there anyway it might be just as well serve a double purpose and we could use the bucket instead of going down the steps to the loo. She dismissed that idea fairly quickly. But almost inevitably it brought back a memory.

When I was a bit of a youth I spent 12 months doing what's called relief milking. You made a commitment to a company that you would be available seven days a week for six months at a time, to go wherever it was required of you, to milk cows. The main purpose was to provide extra help when people were ill or on holiday but as time went on you also found yourself on farms where the farmers were so difficult/awkward/or just plain miserable, that no one would work for them on a regular basis. Thankfully these farms were in a minority but I did find myself on some.

So it was quite an event for me, turning up on that first farm. I arrived on Sunday evening and the farmer's son was due to go on holiday the next day. I was to sleep in the farmhouse and they first showed me my room and then took me into their living room where they introduced me to the rest of the family and some friends who were visiting. I was painfully shy at the time, I still am but not quite so painful. I had a cup of tea with them and a piece of cake and made my excuses and went to bed. When I got back on the landing there were about six closed doors 'looking' at me. I could remember which door led to my bedroom, but I couldn't remember which one was the bathroom. The last thing I wanted was for the family to hear me opening and shutting bedroom doors. Ever resourceful, I decided to relieve myself out of the bedroom window. It was dark when I arrived, I'd only been there a couple of hours. How was I to know there was a tin roof just below my window?

10 JANUARY 2015

Christmas sort of sneaked past me this year. Before I could get myself properly grumpy, it had been and gone. I'll make more effort next time. Don't tell anyone but I quite enjoyed it. Thank goodness I can record programmes to watch instead of endless repeats. I watched the film *Babe* twice. As happy endings go, it's got to be right up there with *Pretty Woman* and *Notting Hill*.

As you all know I wanted a dog for Christmas, well to be precise a puppy, to be even more precise a corgi puppy. That was not to be, so I won't dwell on it. But I did get a new dog for two weeks. Some neighbours who live in a barn conversion on the yard were away for two weeks to Florida and they asked me to look after their dog. Use a bit of imagination and it had a sort of connection with a corgi, well, it takes quite a lot of imagination actually. We all know that a corgi is a sort of domesticated fox, so what do I get to look after? An Akita. It's supposed to be a Japanese dog, it looks like a sort of Husky, but it's really a domesticated wolf. I've never had to look after a dog like it. It was totally out of control, which was probably more to do with its life than its breed.

You couldn't let it off its lead or it was away. I know because it got away from me a couple of times and it was gone for two hours. If you caught it again you were just lucky. It made *The Great Escape* look quite amateurish. Of course there's a lot of responsibility involved in looking after someone's dog, all a bit worrying. If it ran loose it could get lost, run over, kill sheep (wolves kill sheep) or, because it is such a lovely dog, get stolen. Anyway we survived, the dog and I. Having a dog to look after (my dogs look after themselves), was a bit reminiscent of having ewes to lamb. Every night, come bedtime and starting to doze off, you had to put your coat on and go out into the dark and the weather to give the dog its walk and do its ablutions. Same again in the morning. Think on reflection I preferred the lambing.

★★★

I like talking to farmers in the pub. Up to a point. They're alright, but it's all sheep, cattle, corn and tractors and hydraulic oil, it only varies according to the time of year, as the seasons progress. My best night for a talk is on Saturday nights when I sit next to my friend the local florist. She's always got good stories to tell. She it is who famously answers unsolicited phone calls from Asian call centres who phone her about changing her electricity supplier by telling them that we don't have electricity around here yet. This answer is beyond the training they have thus far received. It causes huge confusion. Whilst they are struggling to reply she then goes on to ask them if they are going to bring electricity to the area. This is definitely outside their remit. She goes on to tell them that the nearest supply is to the barn in Jones' field which is only about 20 fields away, but if you are calling from India or somewhere just as far away, Jones' barn might as well be on the moon. The call always ends with the call centre hanging up, which has got to be a victory of sorts. I often wonder if they do actually record the conversation for 'training purposes', and if so, what everyone thinks.

Anyway I venture out on Christmas Eve to the pub, and there's a goodly turnout of local people for the occasion. The pub puts on traditional local fare like onion bhajis and spring rolls. Christmas Eve is almost as good as New Year's Eve for getting kisses. You can sometimes get lips on Christmas Eve off people who don't even offer you a cold cheek at any other time. (And that's just the women.) Anyway I'm sitting in my favourite seat next to the florist and I ask her how busy she had been in the shop that Christmas Eve. So she tells me she's had the best Christmas Eve she's had for years. She never gives you a clue about how her business is going but if she says it was good, it was probably very good. I've always thought that if you went in there you paid so much for the flowers and so much for the experience. But I mustn't digress.

She's in full flow, well, she's probably had six brandy and cokes by now, which is always a good investment. She tells me that mid-afternoon she gets this phone call from someone she doesn't know (and she doesn't know where they live) who says she likes the idea of putting a posy of flowers on her Granddad's grave for Christmas. As a dedicated florist, my friend thinks this is a good idea as well, well she would, wouldn't she? So they discuss price, £10, and discuss choice of flowers and agree on both. So my friend says that she closes the shop at five so she'd better collect them soon. But the lady says that she is not local and could the florist put the flowers on the grave for her. So my busy florist, on her own in a busy shop, starts to get alarm signals. So where's the graveyard? It's in the town where the shop is. So that's OK-ish. 'Do you know where the grave is?' 'No I don't.' It's a small local town but there's a very big graveyard. I don't actually know what the florist told the lady on the phone. I just hope it's not what she told us she said.

15 JANUARY 2015

Now that we have become clear of TB and have been clear for the required number of tests, we are back onto a 12-monthly testing regime. It was unwelcome news that turned up with all the Christmas cards that told us that we had got to test all our cattle again before the end of March. This surely means that there has been a TB outbreak on a nearby farm. If you look at this objectively, and you probably should, it's sensible stuff. If the long-term aim is to clear up the TB problem, extra testing in the locality of an outbreak appears to be sensible. But only just. I don't know where the other outbreak is. I will only know if the affected farmers choose to tell me. I could, if I knew where the problem was, plan next summer's grazing accordingly.

I have parcels of land in three different locations and therefore quite a lot of neighbours. I've just tried to count our fields: there are 24. All but five of them are next to a wood. The five that are not are only a field away from a wood. There's badgers in all the woods. I don't know how many because if I went out with a lamp at night to count them it could easily be interpreted that I was out to kill them. There's people out there who would just love to see a farmer locked up for that, put in the slammer as we say around here.

So I have got to present my cattle for testing by the end of March. By the end of April, those same cattle would be grazing next to badgers that have TB. So what's the point of all that? No point at all. Within the wider scheme of things it would be common sense to TB test some of the badgers as well. But common sense in this matter is in short supply.

And it gets worse. So it's OK for my cattle to graze next to infected badgers. Infected badgers clearly need culling. But there is a general election the following month, in May. An election that is as difficult to read as any for generations. So we come to the 'what ifs'. What if the next election produces another hung parliament, which seems the likely scenario. If we have the same party alliance again, then what we have at present is not good enough as regards TB because it is reluctant to roll out badger culling to a wider area. We know for sure that if the Labour Party is involved, culling will finish. What we don't know is what the UKIP view on TB is. To be fair to them, they probably don't know either. If individual candidates were pressed you would probably get a range of views anyway.

What do the SNP think of the TB issue? They've probably not given it much thought but they could have a big say after the election. TB is not a big issue in Scotland and you can be sure that the SNP will want things to stay that way, and I don't blame them. So the big picture, the long-term vision on TB, has never been so misted up.

But there are things I do know. I know that farmers have had enough, dairy farmers with low milk prices in particular. A combination of a milk price below the cost of production and a TB outbreak could probably spell the end for a lot of hard-working dairy farmers. Come the summer I think that there could be a badger cull. I think it will be going on everywhere. I think that farmers will do it quietly on their own farms. The anti-cull activists won't have a clue how to stop it because it will be so big they won't know which way to turn. The irony is that I think that politicians know this full well. I think that they will criticise it in public. But in private they will welcome a solution to a problem they have failed to grasp.

★★★

There's a B road runs alongside our village. At right angles to that runs a quieter road that is really the main road for the village itself. A small stream runs the length of this road. It makes for a very nice feature. There's no grassy bank between stream and road, there's the road and there's the stream. Lots of cottages and houses are on the other side of the stream. The foundations of some houses form the banks of the stream and cars and pedestrians cross little bridges to get over it. We're only talking about 4ft wide, and the stream is only a couple of feet below the road level. You get to the village hall up this road. Cars leaving late night dances have, on occasion, found themselves in the stream!

Trout can be seen in the stream. We get reports of trout at the pub. 'We ought to tickle a few,' says someone. Immediately I sense possibilities. I tell them I bought my first car with the proceeds of tickled trout. Never tickled one in my life but that's just a technicality, I have the audience's wide-eyed attention and respect. 'There's only one time to tickle a trout,' I tell them, 'between 11 and 12 at night, at that time they will roll over on their backs to be tickled.' Glances are exchanged. In their minds they are selling fish and changing cars. Between 11 and 12 is the time they weave their way home from the pub past the stream. I'll report back to you.

24 JANUARY 2015

There was a time in my life that I used to meet gamekeepers on a regular basis. I used to buy their shot game and export it to France. Twenty years ago, the bane of a gamekeeper's life were poachers. Night after night they would have to go out on 'poacher watch'. Long cold hours out until the early hours of the morning, just in case someone was after their pheasants. I'm sure that keepers are never paid overtime. Poachers could vary between the solitary local out for one for the pot, or a gang who might clear out a covert.

Always at the back of the keeper's mind would be the

possibility of physical confrontation. With the lone local poacher it would also be a battle of wits. I always suspected that for the lone poacher the challenge this presented would be just as important as the possible pheasant prize. If there was a gang involved, there would probably be a fight. Lots of keepers usually have lots of dogs, a dog for different purposes, bit like a golfer and his bag of clubs. Most keepers in those days had a big nasty dog, for their own protection.

I never hear now of keepers out on poacher watch. There are so many pheasants shot these days, especially on large-scale commercial shoots, that a pheasant today has little value. So if you are inclined to a bit of poaching, why would you go out in the early hours looking for a pheasant when you can buy one around here, oven ready, at the butchers for £3.50? Shooting is often justified by saying that everything that is shot, is eaten. On small shoots it is, but on a very large shoot that is debatable. A huge bag of birds might be collected by the game dealer but I suspect that only the best are eaten. It's all about perceptions.

★★★

On Boxing Day, I was watching the news on television. They were visiting hunt kennels prior to traditional Boxing Day meets. Supporters were struggling to find the right words to justify what they were doing. What people really need to say is 'I go hunting or shooting because I enjoy it.' It's that simple. But presumably, unacceptable. So they have to search for specious arguments that are just a bit leaky. Anyway if gamekeeping is anything like farming, if you get rid of one problem it is soon replaced by another.

So what has replaced poachers as the keeper's challenge? I suspect it's foxes. A keeper's year begins when he starts to get his pens ready for a new consignment of poults. It will be mid-July and at night he will go out with lamps and rifle to 'clear up' the foxes. Foxes are despatched at this time of year in huge numbers yet they still keep coming. They continue to thrive as a species. The irony is that they are probably flourishing because there are so many pheasants about, providing them with a 12-month-a-year food supply.

Nevertheless, I'm still surprised there are so many foxes about. I saw three on the road one night returning from the pub, three in 1½ miles. Stephen was scraping the yards one morning after milking. It was still dark but the yard lights shine down the adjoining fields for about 30 or 40 yards. Either side of a fence he could see what he took to be my dog Mert and David's young collie bitch. Mert is mostly nocturnal now (it was still night, but only just). They were either side of a fence and running up and down it. When it gets lighter he can see it is two foxes. They eventually get together and are still running about playing when he finishes, they are only 30 yards away and completely ignore him.

★★★

There's a lady of my acquaintance who comes in the pub about once a week. Had a bad back, this lady, for several weeks now. She tells me about this bad back every time we see her. Not getting better at all, her back. But help is at hand. A builder who comes in regularly tells us that he often has back problems. Just when we, the rest of us, think we are about to be regaled with bad back stories all evening, he tells the lady that he has a wide body belt that he wears whenever he is thus afflicted and that seems to do the trick every time.

They arrange that she should borrow it, which she does. And it seems to be helping her. Now the only discussion we have is whether she should wear it over her thermal vest or under it. Which some people seem to find quite interesting.

Her husband comes in limping Tuesday night. He tells us a big oak tree has blown down in the gales and he was walking along the trunk cutting the boughs off when he fell off and the chainsaw fell on top of him. Some people think this serves him right because he's always bragging that he has the biggest chainsaw in the parish. He's hurt his back as well as his leg so we recommend that he use the body belt as well as his wife. But there's only one belt so it is suggested that when they go to bed, they put the body belt around the two of them. Everyone is quite taken with this idea. Especially as his wife is quite a bit larger than he is. It is suggested that he would be wriggling about like a little lamb that has just had a rubber ring put on its tail. Not a place for sympathy, the pub.

31 JANUARY 2015

So I'm reading the 'Countryside' section of *Western Daily Press*, 10th January, and I find the comment 'some retailers are paying above the market price [for milk] and treat their farmers well.' This makes me so angry. This has got to be one of the biggest cons of all time. The fact of the matter is that the statement is true. But it has to be put into some sort of context. Major retailers have dairy farms that are dedicated to supply them with milk. They pay them a price based on cost of production and to leave a reasonable margin. But the milk that goes into these dedicated supplies is only 16% of the UK production. So 84% of the milk and dairy products in your retailer don't qualify for this largesse. But the farmers who supply the dedicated milk tend to be larger and better invested so it's probably only 10% of dairy farmers who benefit. They are presently receiving around 32 pence per litre for their milk. The rest of us, the 90%, only get around 23ppl. I'm actually on just over 20p! So what's in it for the supermarkets? Well it's obvious isn't it! When dairy farmers complain about low milk prices, just like I am doing now, they can hold their hands up and say, 'It's not me, I pay my farmers well,' and they do, but it's only 16% of what they buy. It's the sort of sleight of hand that you would expect from these people. It's just so worrying that some journalists are taken in by it all.

Yesterday I took two beef cross bull calves to market. I was really pleased with the prices they made. At one time we would suckle our beef cross calves on their mums for about three days to give them a good start and then put them onto milk powder which was cheaper and their mum's milk would go into the tank where it was intended.

Since milk prices crashed we've kept these calves on their mothers for five weeks. At five weeks, on ad lib mother's milk, you get a fit, strong, well-fleshed calf that is full of it. A bit like a teenage boy going out on a Friday night. When I started farming I thought that there would always be a living for someone producing nature's most natural, balanced nutritious food. It's a sad irony that we have reached the point that I am now better off putting that milk into a calf rather than the tank for the people for whom it was intended.

★★★

I've been troubled with my knees for some years now. It's not difficult to find reasons for this. Too much rugby for too long. Too much tug of war! But the main factor is probably a lifetime of walking about on cold concrete in wellies. Just to prove this latter theory, several years ago I had to have keyhole surgery on the worst knee. It was an in-and-out job on the same day but I had to have a general anaesthetic. So I went to an orthopaedic hospital and they put me on a spare bed in a ward to prepare me. There were ten men already in bed in the ward, they'd all had new knees and seven of them were dairy farmers!

Anyway, I'm having physiotherapy on my knee at the moment. I'm not yet at the stage where I need new knees (thank goodness), but I'm having to do exercises that will hopefully tighten up all my leg muscles which in turn will tighten up on the wear and tear on my knees. In addition to my legs, the lady wants me to exercise by doing some 'pelvic tilting rotation' using my lateral abdominal wall, she says that this will improve my inner self. I tell her I go to the pub to do that usually, but she's not impressed. I tell her I find some of the leg lifting exercises very easy, so she says I should buy some weights that I can strap around my ankles, and she shows me some she has. I try them and the idea is OK. But do I need to be buying special ankle weights? No I don't. So I put a swede in a plastic bag and put my feet through the handles.

7 FEBRUARY 2015

If you are anti-shooting you probably won't like what I am about to write. If you are pro-shooting you probably won't like it either, you'd probably prefer that I didn't tell the story. But the story has, in my opinion, quite an amazing end to it, and you have to tell the whole story to get the picture.

Occasionally when pheasant shooting takes place, some birds are not killed by the shot, they are possibly winged. It's not many birds that are affected and these birds will alight on the ground and run for cover. That's why they are called runners. The people who are shooting know this may happen and will go to extraordinary lengths to catch these birds so that they can be despatched humanely.

On bigger shoots, people called 'pickers up' are stationed well behind the line of guns, with their excellent dogs, and are always on top of the job. If a bird eludes them they will spend ages and literally go for miles in search of an injured bird. At this point I suspect some of you are saying, 'So they should.' Well, I can assure you, 'So they do.'

On smaller less formal shoots, everything comes to a halt while everyone searches for the lost bird. Mind it's not all that it seems sometimes. At the end of a drive you can ask a 'gun' how he got on and he might say, 'I've got ten down in the wood behind me.' So dogs will be despatched and people will struggle through undergrowth and after about half an hour of searching you might have found two or three. The other seven or eight were never shot in the first place but some people always like to appear better than they are, I expect you've noticed that.

Next time you ask the same man how he got on and he says that there are ten or twelve behind him, you say to yourself, 'I bet there are,' but you still make the effort to find them.

I've been at shoots where the man who collects the game will ask the guns how many birds they think they have shot, he'll add all the numbers up and it sometimes comes to twice the number he has on the game cart!

I've never been a fan of shooting huge numbers. I haven't shot for years but I can still remember individual good shots I have made from 20 years ago. My greatest pleasure always came from having a good gun dog, one that would seek out the game: I would shoot it (hopefully) and the dog would retrieve it.

I once bought an adult spaniel called Bullet off a gamekeeper. He was probably the best gun dog I ever had. I was in a small informal shoot at the time. There was a good crowd of us who all played rugby together. We used to have a lot of fun and at the end of the season we would have an awards dinner and Bullet always won the dog of the year award. He was as good a gun dog as any on the shoot but he had a speciality. We used to stop for a sandwich in an old barn at midday and sit in a circle on some bales. At every shoot there would be a guest or two and Bullet would sit in the middle of the circle as half soaked as you like. The regulars amongst us always knew what was about to happen.

A guest would be telling some shooting story or other and in emphasising his own eloquence his hand would stray just a bit too far into the centre of the circle. With a speed that you could barely register, the sandwich within the hand would be on its way down Bullet's throat. And Bullet would be sitting there totally unconcerned, as if nothing had happened.

Shooting is a bit like most things in life, who has got the best dog, gun, clothing, 4x4, this even manifests itself at lunchtime. Out would come the stainless steel flasks of soup and wicker hampers with sandwiches and meat pies. (I always had bread and cheese in a sliced loaf wrapper. I suppose that was inverted snobbery.) One day a very pretentious guest had a really nice piece of Camembert, Bullet had that as well. Anyway, back to the story.

Duck shooting. I don't much like duck shooting on a large scale. Mallards can become very tame very quickly. They become so tame when they are fed every day, that they often refuse to fly off the sanctuary of the water where they live. Shots are sometimes fired in the air to flush them off. I knew of one large shoot where they had to buy some radio controlled toy boats to chase the ducks around to try to get them to fly.

I've shot at ducks, I like eating wild duck. The ducks get off the lake or pond and everyone shoots at them, but the ducks fly off a fair way and then they start flying back home again. So everybody has another shot at them, which I would never do. Seems to me you've had one chance and that should be that. It's a bit like fox hunting. Why do they dig foxes out after they have gone to earth? The fox has beaten you today, let him live, he's won.

Anyway it's time to return to my original theme, wounded birds. A wounded pheasant will land on the ground and run. A duck will, if it can, land back on water and swim. The same efforts will be made to recover this wounded bird, usually by sending dogs into the water to retrieve it. Mostly this is very effective but sometimes if a duck is still full of fight it will wait until the dog is close at hand and then dive underwater to escape.

And finally, I get to the purpose of all this story. There's a black Labrador lives in our village that is very good at retrieving shot ducks off water. But when he gets up close to a wounded bird and that bird dives down underwater to escape, the dog will dive down underwater to catch it. It will dive down with such vigour that it will disappear completely from sight. I've never ever heard of a dog swimming underwater before. It doesn't only swim underwater, it catches the duck underwater as well. [I went down the road one day in a rush to attend to a sick cow a few miles away. I forgot Bullet was loose. He followed me, 50 yards behind, and was tragically clipped by a lorry].

14 FEBRUARY 2015

A very good friend, of many years' standing, had one of those big birthdays recently. We'd met playing rugby and there were lots of our rugby players there. Some of them I'd not seen for 20–30 years, but they had all made an effort to attend because the man with the birthday is a big character as well as a good friend to us all. So it was not just a surprise birthday party, it was a grand reunion as well. And as usual I'm watching what is going on and reflecting on it all and I'm thinking of just how lucky we all were to play sport together.

There's a complete cross-section of society there, people from all walks of life. All these people were totally at ease with each other. At the time in their lives when they had been regular companions, they would have had an insight into the trials and tribulations of each others' lives which would have established an empathy which still exists today.

And every Saturday afternoon they would go out to do battle together and in the evening there would be fun. It's possibly only team sport that does this. I once knew three rugby players who formed what they call the back row at a very good standard rugby club. These three played as a unit together for about 12 years and were so good at what they did together they became quite famous within that sporting environment. They were known as the three D's. Doctor, dentist and dustman.

When you have that sort of reunion it is inevitable that people start reminiscing. We were talking about the first time our club went on Easter tour. Rugby players at our level don't seem to get that sort of fun these days, all their Saturdays are taken up with league fixtures. We went to the Isle of Wight. We used to have a very good team in those days and we were strengthened by the outstanding rugby-playing students we had, who were home from college for the holiday. We went in a big minibus and fitted four barrels in the very back and the pipes led up to the front and the beer tap was on the dashboard. We were only 13 of us who went, two short of a full side, so for our first game we got two players off the touchline. We didn't make that mistake again, and played three more matches two short, but at least we knew where we were. We won all four of our matches.

Anyway, one afternoon we were walking back to our boarding house after a game and one of the students was telling someone, who had been his teacher only 12 months before, that he was now studying geology and was already something of an expert. We were walking through a suburb and passing quite a large imposing house with a very large garden. There was a dry stone wall that was the boundary of the property. It was over 6ft high where we were passing and tapered down to about 3ft about 30 yards down the road. So the teacher said to the student, 'If you know so much about geology, what sort of rock is this?' And as he said it he pulled out a piece of stone from the wall, honestly it was no bigger than half a house brick and quite loose. With that the whole wall went down like a row of dominoes for its entire length. It went down with such force there was turf off the lawn lying in the road. Boy did we run.

★★★

I'm glad the shooting season has finished. The shooting season leaves a social vacuum in my life. I like to go to the pub on Saturday night (you may have noticed that). Normally I go at about nine o'clock, so do most of my friends. Trouble is, most of my friends go beating or shooting on Saturdays. This means they get into the pub between 4 and 5pm. The plan is that they will have a few drinks and something to eat and go home at 7pm to get changed and come back out at 9pm. Like most plans, this rarely works. Fortified by hip flask and port all day, besides what they have in the pub, they go home and rarely reappear. Sometimes they stay at the pub until I arrive by which time they are incoherent.

So a friend is telling me she's going out on Saturday night and leaves a meal for her husband for when he gets home from shooting.

When she gets home he is sitting in his armchair with the plate on his lap. The plate is pristine clean, so she knows that the dog has had his dinner. His arms are outstretched on the arms of the chair and the knife and fork are held pointing vertically in the air. He is fast asleep and snoring, he even has a mouthful in his mouth.

21 FEBRUARY 2015

Today, as I write, I have yet to see a new year lamb. As harbingers of spring go, this year's lambs have got to be right up there with daffodils. I know people who have got lambs already but I haven't seen them, so it doesn't count. It's a sign of farming and the way it is going.

Years ago lots of people would produce early lamb for the good trade that would be, traditionally, for Easter. To do this you needed to try to lamb your ewes, as many as you could, in December. Some breeds are more suited to this than others. Suffolk ewes, large, black-faced sheep, would do the job admirably. There was always the possibility of a downside. If the three or so months preceding Easter were bad, weatherwise, you might end up having to purchase everything that the ewe and the lamb need to eat. If there were weeks of frosts and snow this would be so expensive that there would be very little margin. That's probably why lambs in a field at this time of year are becoming a more rare sight.

I have a friend who would lamb 500 Suffolk ewes early every year and who did a good job of it. These days he lambs all his ewes in April. The ewes milk well on the grass, the lambs are getting grass as well as milk and he is making more money for a lot less work and trouble. It's a route that all branches of agriculture are being driven down. Try to keep your costs down because what you produce will buy you less and less of your inputs.

A friend of mine put this into context. He was telling me that in 1976, the year of the very dry summer, he was selling potatoes for £200 a ton. This year he is getting £70 and he says he has to be very careful when he grades them. The slightest blemish, and even at that price, he could get a load rejected. '£200 a ton 30 years ago and now we are expected to manage at £70,' he tells me indignantly. 'It could even be 40 years ago,' I tell him. I always try to help people along life's difficult road if I can. He thinks about this for a minute while he works it out. 'That's right, it's 40 years,' and he raises his indignation level accordingly.

He always has a pallet on his yard with a few bags of potatoes on, his retail outlet, and an honesty box in case no one's about. 'Even at this price we get the odd bag pinched.' And his indignation goes into a range of vocabulary that's not suitable to print here.

28 FEBRUARY 2015

I'm not sure how the conversation started, probably on licensed premises. But the new incumbents at our local pub report strange doings. Twice, one of the employees has reported being tapped on the shoulder and has turned around to find no one there! Someone else said that they were coming up the cellar steps and someone crossed past the doorway above them. On each occasion the person involved was the only person in the pub!

A friend of mine says, continuing on the same theme, that she was taking a short cut across the churchyard at dusk after putting some flowers on a grave, and someone was standing in the church doorway. She went across to have a word, thinking it was the church warden locking up for the night, but by the time she got there, there was no one there. She reckons she ran all the way home, which if you saw her, would be a sight in itself.

Did you ever hear the story (this is one of my digressions), about when they put new poles in for the telephone lines in our village? They put one right in the angle of the churchyard walls. As the pole itself was on an angle, they had to put in one of those wire stays to brace it up. The wire stay went very close to a fresh grave.

So a bit of a character in the village announces in the pub, 'I see old Fred has had the telephone put in.'

Anyway, back to strange doings. My daughter lives in a wonderful old farmhouse, it's called a castle but it's probably a sort of fortified manor house. There are parts of it that go back to the 12th century. It's got all the history associated with it that you would expect from something of that age. You are not advised to go onto her lawn and put your foot through a molehill, there could be a cannonball in it! You enter their yard through an archway that reputedly once housed a drawbridge. I'm not seeking to be pretentious, it's a working rented farm, it just happens to have all this history to it.

Anyway, legend has it that a young girl was crushed in this archway by a wagon or a carriage 2–300 years ago. She was taken into a bedroom in the house where she died a few days later. Now here's the strange thing.

My daughter provides farmhouse B&B, and on several occasions guests have come down to breakfast and reported having seen this girl. They've not been told the story beforehand (telling people your house is haunted is not necessarily something you would put on your website). The guests could well be 12 months apart, would be totally unconnected, the 'girl' only appears to men, they know that her name is Veronique and that she had bad teeth!

But that's not the half of it, there's more to come. You know the story of the two little princes in the tower don't you? Well, another legend has it that the two little boys spent the night there on their way to Ludlow Castle and eventually the Tower of London. And other B&B guests have come down to breakfast and reported hearing children crying in their room, during the night. They hadn't been told the 'princes' story either, there could have been months apart in their visits, and they had certainly never met. So what's all that about?

I might as well keep going now I have started. When my daughter moved there she put a picture of some tulips, that she liked, on the wall. Quite regularly she would find the picture on the floor in the morning. The nail would still be in the wall and the string would be intact. In the end she got fed up and the picture is in a cupboard. (We're getting to the end now.) So one day a lady turns up for B&B and my daughter shows her to her bedroom and her bathroom and the woman starts acting very strange and says that she doesn't think she can stay there. 'Oh dear, is there anything wrong with the accommodation?' 'No, it's just that I am a psychic and I'm picking up on some really strange and violent vibes.'

You, the reader, may interpret this as you will, it may be that an uncharitable thought has occurred to you. I won't agree with you because I'm a much kinder person. So my daughter explains about the story of Veronique but says the guest has nothing to fear because she only appears to men. She doesn't tell her about the two princes. Breakfast the next day is a revelation. The lady says she has seen Veronique in the night. So my daughter says 'but she only appears to men'. 'Ah,' says the lady, 'but in a previous life I was a soldier in the 17th century. That's why she appeared to me.' OK – in retrospect I'll agree with you, she was crazy. And 'Veronique' had told the lady guest that she was once in love with a Dutchman who treated her very badly and that somewhere in the house there was a picture of some tulips and she couldn't bear to see it because it reminded her of Holland and as a consequence the unfaithful Dutchman. So I'm starting to get sceptical myself now, I can't work out how a young girl with bad teeth, living near Craven Arms, would manage to pull a Dutchman, 2-300 years ago? The lady guest has also seen the two little boys.

Me, I don't believe a word of it. It's all coincidental nonsense. I doubt if you will read any of this anyway. I'm writing it in bed, the duvet is pulled up over my head, I've got a torch with me, and my handwriting is terrible.

7 March 2015

Ever since a local lady put on Facebook that there were lots of brown hares to be seen off the footpaths that cross my top land, the hares' lives have been in jeopardy. I told her at the time that I was disappointed with what she had done. She replied that other people had as much right to see the hares as I did. Unfortunately, 'other people' includes hare coursers and poachers. There's a group up there quite regularly now. There's eight of them with 11 dogs, rifles and what they call laser lamps. The hares don't stand a chance. The police are not interested, 'If you shot all the hares, they wouldn't come.' What a dreadful response. Such an easy solution for them. If someone were after badgers there would be cars and helicopters everywhere. So who decides that such a lovely inoffensive creature as a brown hare doesn't matter? There's no end to the damage that naive people can do to the countryside.

★★★

Ever since before Christmas we've had 40 to 50 what we call big cattle, and dry cows and in calf heifers, outside. They have been outside eating stubble turnips and fodder beet and a big bale of hay a day or, latterly, some silage. They've done really well and thrived. We've got a shed close at hand and we would fetch them in on some of those worst nights of snow and rain, but for most of the time, outside is where they have been. The numbers vary because some have had to come home to calve and other cows have gone into their dry period and gone to join those outside. Now, at the end of February, they are starting to calve on a regular basis so we get them in every night. They come when we call them, keen for a warm dry night on their straw bed, but when we loose them out next morning, they march off up the field, really keen to get to the root crops.

Traditionally, say 40-50 years ago, keeping stock outside in the winter on root crops was the tool for successfully maintaining fertility on this local, high, light land. Of course it was done by folding sheep on root crops but I like to think we are doing the same thing with cattle.

My son doesn't like sheep. I think that if I went off one day and bought a trailer load of sheep, he wouldn't say anything, he'd help me to unload them, but he'd be gone next morning. I always used to think that those shepherds who had to fold sheep on roots in winter had a hard life. They might travel up there on a tractor but I doubt if it had a heater, in fact it might not have a cab at all or at best a canvas one. They wouldn't have access to the sort of warm, weather-proof clothing that we take for granted today. It was a cold wet life.

The fences that contained the sheep would be wire netting held up with willow stakes that they had fashioned themselves. The shepherds around here didn't use sledgehammers to drive the posts in, because they might split the stakes. They all had what they called, I think, a stake beedle. It was made out of ash, the limb of the ash would be the handle and the sort of club end would come out of a bigger part of the tree that had been hollowed out so that it fitted over the end of the stake as it hit it. It was all a part of a sort of frugal culture they had, the stakes and the way they made things themselves: what you don't buy, you don't pay for.

Sheep are still folded on root crops, swedes and turnips, but it's a lot easier job these days. It's done quickly and fairly easily with electric fencing. Sometimes the electric fencing paraphernalia is mounted onto a quad bike so that it is laid out or reeled in very quickly. I know a farmer who has a lot of sheep on roots at different locations and two or three of the family will go off for the whole day moving electric fences to give the sheep a patch of fresh roots. One of them was telling me the other day, 'We don't take sandwiches when we are moving fences on the turnips, we just take bread and butter.' 'Why is that?' 'We cut a slice of turnip and put it in the bread and butter, it saves using jam or cheese.' It seems frugality lives in their DNA.

★★★

It's the lull before lambing starts around here. The shooting stories are all told and retold. There will be plenty of sheepy stories quite soon but in the meantime in the pub we have to recycle some old ones. Here we go, someone says that the obituaries in the local paper are running to four pages. The same person said the same thing last year. Off we go with undertaker jokes. Locally we have John the Box and his son Phil the Hole. Nearby there are Sid the Lid and Keith the Wreath. Most undertakers around here are builders as well. I'm not sure which part of their dual occupation comes first, which is the vocation. At first sight it seems a strange combination but it is possibly because the builder could turn his hand to making coffins. Most of them have gone a bit more upmarket these days. They have to compete with very professional undertakers that operate in the larger towns. So they hire in a hearse for the day. It's not many years ago that your hearse could be a Transit van or a Volvo estate! We are told of one local undertaker who used to really love making coffins. He loved it so much that he would have half a dozen readymade at any time. So, apparently, he would be called out to someone's house at the time of a bereavement, he would measure up the deceased and sometimes he would say, 'Sorry, I haven't got a coffin to fit, you will have to call someone else.'

14 MARCH 2015

I was recently writing about harbingers of spring. I've seen daffodils very early this year but it was my failure to see a lamb that had prompted my thoughts. Well, I've seen a lamb now, but I had to go out of my way to seek one out, just in order to tick it off my list. So I thought I was well up to date in the 'harbinger' department. Yesterday I was carting farmyard manure (we don't call it that), it will be spread and ploughed in for this year's root crops later on. Suddenly I discovered that I wasn't alone in the tractor cab. My companion was a big fat wasp. Wasps usually turn up here much later – if they are to be a harbinger, it's usually to tell you that the plums are getting ripe. Where he had come from his slumbers I'm not sure. What I am sure about is that he was very, very grumpy indeed. I opened the windows and doors and he was soon on his way. I don't know how many mistakes a wasp makes in his lifetime but it was very frosty here last night. I suspect that this was his last mistake.

★★★

Sheep are funny things, you either love them or hate them. If you love them, and most people who keep them do, they are your life. Your whole life revolves around the needs of your sheep and how those needs evolve as the seasons of the year themselves evolve. The whole focus of your life is on sheepy matters: it might be on lambing, perhaps buying some new young ewes in the autumn, almost certainly buying some fresh rams (tups), all the while making sure you had some good dogs and some good pups (that should make good dogs) in the pipeline. Then before you know where you are it's time to scan your ewes to see how many lambs they are carrying and the whole cycle begins again.

The sheep for their part will spend the whole year trying to undo all of your best efforts. They will try to die at every opportunity. But failing that they will do their best to succumb to all the sheep diseases known to man (or should that be sheep), they will try to escape, they will fight you every step of the way. So if you happen to see a farmer leaning on a gate surveying a fine flock of sheep, don't for a second underestimate the effort that he has put in to achieve what is running about in the field.

I know a man (have you noticed that I always seem to know a man? I try to give the characters in my stories anonymity, but if you lived around here you would know immediately who I am talking about). So he's got a lot of ewes, probably 1,000, no one but him really knows. The sheep spend their summers on a high hill he owns, which is split into four or five huge fields. He's a good case of the 'living' for his sheep. He's probably not spent a night off the farm for 20 or 30 years. He goes to market and sheep sales in the summer, but wherever he goes off for the day, it's only after he's been around the sheep.

Every day, when the sheep are on the hill in the summer, he sets off on his quad bike to do his rounds. There will be two dogs riding with him on the bike and probably two more running alongside. He will have with him all the injections and equipment for treating most problems he is likely to come across in the normal course of events and his dogs are so good that he can catch any sheep that is ailing, no matter how big the fields. He never leaves his sheep until he is satisfied that all is OK.

There are several footpaths that cross his land and it is quite common for walkers to knock on his back door, Sunday afternoons are a particular time for this, to tell him that there is a sheep up on the hill that is limping. It's always fascinated me, this phenomenon. If someone is visiting a hospital and sees a child limping out of A & E, they don't phone the hospital or the NSPCC to complain that the child has been refused treatment do they? They assume that the child has been treated and that it will get better in the fullness of time. If an animal is involved, everyone assumes neglect. And if you aspire to care for your animals as I do, and the vast majority of farmers do, and as the man in my story certainly does, it can be particularly galling to be told how to look after them by someone who clearly knows nothing about it.

And even in this case where there are probably 1,000 ewes and 12-1400 lambs up there, no matter how vigilant you are, there could always be one that is limping. But not to worry, these Sunday afternoon calls need not be too much of an inconvenience. So my man enquires of his visitors, visitors that have gone a long way out of their way to seek him out, if the afflicted sheep happens to have a blue mark on it. And they say yes. 'Ah well, I caught that one this morning and I dressed its foot and gave it an injection and it should be fine by morning, but I'll look out for it to make sure it's OK. And that's why I marked it.' And off they go, well satisfied with themselves and what they've done. And the farmer goes back to his armchair. He smiles to himself; he knows that the visitors who took him to task know nothing at all about sheep. There's over 2,000 sheep up on his hill and every single one has a blue mark on it.

21 MARCH 2015

I'm in the pub and the talk is of lambing. A friend of mine who is a lady (nearly wrote 'a lady friend of mine') is telling us how their lambing is going. Her husband is with us but he's not saying a lot, he's got a full time job just trying to keep his eyes open. They've got some ewes that are lambing in some buildings a mile from where they live and he and his son take it in turns to stay there the night in a caravan that they have. Eventually he perks up enough to tell us that he gets out of the caravan every hour to check the ewes, that they've had a good lambing and his biggest problem thus far seems to be that he can only get ITV on the little television he has in the caravan.

So we tease him a bit about how sophisticated the living arrangements are in the caravan which we all know are on the rough side of rough. So I enquire of him (innocently) if he gets dressed every time he goes around the sheep or does he go around them in his pyjamas, knowing full well that he keeps a heater on full time to keep the caravan warm and that he stays fully dressed all night and that in all probability he keeps his wellies on when he gets under the duvet to sleep.

It's his wife's turn again now and she tells us she has bought him a onesie that looks like a sheep and that he gets on his hands and knees to go around the sheep and they assume that he is another sheep, so that he can check on the ewes without disturbing them. Of course this isn't true and we don't believe her but his protestations are very amusing. He's so indignant about the whole thing that he becomes as awake as he has been all evening. Which is all part of the fun.

I don't have lady friends but there is a group that I call 'carers'. They are all ladies and there's about five of them. They do a lot of the important little things in my life, like going to fetch the drinks when it's my round and holding my hands when I go down some awkward steps. They don't seem to have worked out that I can negotiate life quite well when they are not about, but you'll not hear any complaint from me.

28 MARCH 2015

For years I used to go to a ladies' hairdressers to have my hair cut, I still do, but this previous one was quite posh and quite big. I'm not sure how I came to go here, it could be I had to take my daughter there before she could drive. I used to quite like it. The boss was a man and all his female assistants used to call him Mr ___, which wasn't his real name. I knew what his real name was because he was born in the next village. I used to have the shampoo and cut and if you were lucky, on a good day, you might get a careless bosom pressed into the back of your neck.

Anyway, I was in the town one day and passing the hairdresser I thought I might as well have a trim while I'm in the area, so I popped my head through the door and the boss's wife was on duty, so I called out 'Any chance of a quickie?' and she said 'Would ten minutes be OK?' And I said, 'Fine, but could I have a haircut afterwards?' All the ladies having their hair done thought it was very amusing.

I do have hairdressing experience of my own. For about 12 years we had a local man, and friend, living in a caravan on our yard. He'd nearly fallen through life's net because of his issues with drink. Falling through a net and landing on our yard is not necessarily a good thing. An evening out for him would be ten pints and ten drinks out of the optics on what he called the top shelf. Which makes the rest of us look quite sensible.

Anyway, I used to cut his hair. It wasn't a particularly

challenging style to accomplish, he liked it shaved right off. I used
to do it with the cow clippers which had sometimes been used for
clipping cows the same day. In fact my biggest problem was often
the streaks of cow muck that the clippers would leave on his head.
But he couldn't see them could he?

Anyway, one summer evening I'm having my tea and he
knocks on the door and asks if I will cut his hair before he goes
to the pub. So I ask him if he will hang on for ten minutes until I
finish my tea. Five minutes later there's another knock on the door.
I open it and there's a salesman there that I don't know, and my
man is still hovering in the background. I can see he is getting a bit
twitchy about getting to the pub. The salesman is launching into
his sales spiel, he looks as if he's a new salesman, and he's wearing
a suit, which salesmen around farms don't do. It's as if he has just
completed his training and his sales pitch is rehearsed and now he's
started he can't stop.

We always treat visitors with courtesy and respect but I
can't get a word in, so I beckon him to follow me. The three of us
go up the yard and around the corner and to the workshop. I get
a 5-gallon drum and Jimmy, who lives up the yard and knows the
form, sits on it. Neither Jimmy or I have spoken thus far but we
have this background noise of sales patter, I think he was selling
minerals. I wrestle the cow clippers out of a box where they are
sleeping amongst some spanners, I get the extension lead and plug
it all in. I get behind Jimmy, and give the clippers a couple of wipes
on my overalls. The salesman is still rattling away but I can see by
his eyes that I have his full attention. I switch on. Jimmy has about
an inch of hair all over his head. I put the three-inch clipper head at
the nape of his neck and take a swipe of hair off all the way up the
back right to his forehead. At about the halfway point the salesman
stops talking. His eyes are wide open, as is his mouth. Jimmy has a
three inch shaved strip from front to back. If you had a Mohican,
that's where the strip would be. There's a bit of cow muck in there

so I wipe it off with my elbow. 'There you are Jim, that looks fine.' The salesman looks at me, then he looks at Jim's hair, so I ask him if he wants a bit of a trim while he's here.

Within 30 seconds he's in his car and off down the yard. The look he gives me as he drives past says that he thinks we are mad. He's probably right. I never saw him again. I finish the rest of Jimmy's hair off and give his head a bit of a wipe with some paper towel. He goes to the wing mirror of the truck to have a look. 'What do you think, Jim?' 'Sound,' he says. I go back to the house to finish my tea. Could be a diversification opportunity here. I still go to a lady to have my hair cut. It's nearer and I don't have shampoo. But she gives me a cup of coffee and we have a gossip. It costs £4.90 but I give her £5. It's not a big tip but as I write today, 10p is over half a litre of milk.

4 April 2015

It's another of spring's harbingers, everyone is looking for a magpie. Come the spring, they are all dusting off their Larsen traps in order to catch magpies to act as decoys. It's not always easy to catch the first one, hen eggs will usually do it but it can take time. Once someone has caught one the rest soon follow and the birds are trafficked about the area until everyone has one. I have a friend with two traps who caught over 60 last year, a number you would think would make a difference. Let's hope he catches 60 again because there are magpies everywhere.

★★★

Most people who don't have grandchildren think that I go on about them too much. But the people who do have grandchildren don't have an issue and mostly agree with me that it is one of the very best things that ever happens to you. I've got five (love them as I do, five is enough), and their ages range from eight to 21. And I watch them as they make their way through their lives, and if I think that one of them is struggling a bit, well I try to put extra help in their direction. Sometimes it's a bit of financial help, £20 for a night out (no good giving a teenager a fiver), but it's mostly an effort to boost their morale.

At the different ages they have different needs. The 21-year-old has got most of what he needs in life. He's quite good at sport, he's got a decent car and he's got a lovely girlfriend. He thinks he's quite sophisticated. But not as sophisticated as the eight-year-old grandson who thinks that a pair of overalls like his Dad's and a shepherds crook, so that he can help with the lambing, is living the dream.

The number two boy has just failed his driving test for the second time. Apparently one fail is sort of OK, but two fails is terrible. And he's bust his leg and can't play rugby again this season. And his body language is showing it.

So what does a doting grandad do? He lets him have his ticket for the Wales-Ireland game. Anyone who knows me knows that that is about as good as it gets from me. And he saw a memorable Welsh win so that will be down to me as well. I've got what they call a debenture at the Millennium Stadium that gives you the right to buy the same seat for every game. It's a superb seat just three rows from the front of the middle tier towards the middle of the field. If the players form up for a lineout at the start of the game, just in front of where I sit, you can smell the embrocation.

I've been going to watch Wales play on a regular basis ever since I left school, I very rarely miss a game at Cardiff and there's a group of us mostly go to an away game every year as well. For my grandson, sitting in my 'good' seat, it's a far cry from when I started going to internationals at his age. It was at what they called the old Cardiff Arms Park. There was a North Stand that consisted of a raised seated area on one level with a standing area terraced beneath it. We got there early and found a good place to see, but as it filled up we found we couldn't see at all. We only saw glimpses of the game and we could only see the ball when it was kicked high into the air. We found ourselves gravitating to an area that ran the length of the stand which seemed to have more room to stand in it.

At half time we were to find out why. A lot, or even most, of the people in the stand above would head for the toilets at half time (some of them might have been in the pub)! Whoever had designed the plumbing above us had not got the arithmetic right. So as thousands of bladders were evacuated, the plumbing couldn't cope and the urinals the length of the stand overflowed and the liquid went through the floorboards and cascaded on us standing underneath. (Some of it was still warm but that's probably too much information.) I remember thinking at the time, as the deluge descended and people crushed into the people in front or behind, in order to get away from a very unpleasant soaking, that there was a social comment here. The people who could afford the price of a stand ticket were doing what they were doing on top of the less wealthy beneath.

It's an analogy that lives on today. The wealthy up above you, not in reality getting you unpleasantly wet, but certainly doing it metaphorically. I used to say that we'll get them back 'when the revolution comes'. That's the sort of thing you say when you are young. I don't actually remember a revolution but there must have been one, because now I find myself sitting up there in the best seats as well, and should I so choose, a teenage grandson as well.

11 April 2015

I'm a very simple person. When people I know want an example of simplicity, they often think of me. A simple person is perfectly happy with simple pleasures. And here is a 'for instance'. Just a few years ago I decided that it would be nice (nice and simple), to have a few turkeys about the yard. It's something we've done before, a little self-contained flock of turkeys living free on the yard, sleeping and feeding where they would, to come and go as they pleased. What a nice picture there was in my mind's eye. Three or four hen turkeys out and about, in the cattle sheds on wet days, out on the yard on the dry ones, pecking about industriously for food whenever they could find it (20 tons of cow cake tipped up in a shed is always a popular place). And shepherding the hens along with the utmost courtesy would be the stag. Always mindful of their safety, and if his little harem was approached by cat, dog, man or beast, he would take up a place between them and his hens and puff out his feathers and strut his defiance. I love to see stag turkeys making their displays. For some reason they remind me of a galleon under full sail (not that I've ever seen one except in films), setting sail for the Indies and a cargo of silks and spices. Eventually, as things progressed there would be three or four, maybe more, young turkey poults that would join the family group, they would be cared for by stag and hens and as these things have a way of evolving, the pick of the litter would end up on our kitchen table on Christmas Day.

So we got our band of turkeys and they struggled. Mr Fox wanted to share them with us and he did. I've told you all this before but both you and I need reminding. So the turkeys had to be confined to our old walled garden for their own safety and they had to be shut up every night in their shed. And they couldn't go out every day to forage, you had to go in and feed them and the stags became very aggressive so you had to feed them with a stick, if you follow me. All this is a far cry from the picture that, you may recall, was in my mind's eye, just a few lines ago.

So I left them out onto the yard again to take their chances with the fox. And that was OK, up to a point, they didn't suffer any predation with the fox but there were three stags and two hens, and our yard became a no-go area. There's people live on our yard in barn conversions, they couldn't get out for a walk. If they left their garden gates open and the turkeys went into their gardens, well ,they simply couldn't get out of the house.

It might well be that on reading this you are saying to yourself, 'A few turkeys wouldn't scare me.' Well they scared me, plenty. If I went around the corner of a building and they were there, and I didn't have a stick, I would beat a hasty retreat until I found one.

Early autumn we caught the stags and put them in a pheasant pen in the woods and they became an amusing spectacle and hazard for the shooters, all of which I have reported previously. So now we have two hen turkeys on the yard and, after the residents discover that they are not a threat, peace returns. The hen turkeys are friendly, they are not a problem, they like to sleep on people's garden furniture and if they yawn in the night, the sensors switch the outside lights all on. One man has two motorboats moored in his garden (which haven't been on water for three years), and they sometimes perch on the cockpits to sleep. He wasn't best pleased about that, especially about having to scrub off turkey poo. I'm not bothered, and in any case, he should shut his garden gate.

But it's spring, isn't it, and hen turkeys' thoughts turn to love. If you walked past them they would squat down in front of you, which is hen turkey speak for come and get me. They would prostrate themselves in front of moving tractors, cars, lorries, dogs, whatever.

The sensitive person that I am was keenly aware that they had needs that wouldn't be satisfied as things were. The idea of bringing a stag back into the yard was quickly dismissed for the reasons previously stated. So we caught the hens and took them to join the stag in the woods. They were well loved-up within five minutes, and everything is looking sort of OK. It's true I haven't got my flock of turkeys on the yard because I've tried it and it didn't work.

But if nature takes its course I might still get my Christmas dinner. So enter the scene, the gamekeeper. He quite likes the turkeys in his release pen. He particularly liked their pursuits of his shooters when they went into the pen and how the one 'gun' ended up full length in the mud trying to escape. Yesterday he goes into the pen to put a bag of wheat in their feeder and the five turkeys are variously arranged on the branches of a tree. The hens are highest up the tree, presumably working on a theory that even the most ardent of stag turkeys can't make love on the branch of a tree.

As he passes by the tree, one of the stags launches himself at him, lands on his head, cutting it with his claws, and the keeper goes down on the floor, as does the bag of wheat. He scrambles to his feet but the turkey drives him out of the pen and up the field. You might think that to someone like me who owns Mert the dog that would bite, Neville the cockerel that would fight the world, this would be OK. But the keeper is young and fit and he can't handle the turkeys. What would they do to some children or ramblers? Worse still, what if the landlady walks by?

18 APRIL 2015

So I'm going to our 'other' land and there's a sign to say that the lane will be closed for a day in two weeks' time for road works. It's a very quiet lane, perhaps ten or twelve cars an hour. So I drive on and go around the corner and there's two cars stopped in front of me and three other cars stopped, coming the other way. I'm thinking, I read the date wrong and the road is already closed. And it is closed, but not by the council. My turkeys have broken out of their wood, made their way to the lane, and are standing there defiantly, no one can get past. I told you they were getting out of hand.

★★★

A lot of what I read from newspaper columnists is often comment about current affairs or issues. But it's something I fairly deliberately avoid. My 'rural rambles' are a stroll in the countryside amongst the flora and fauna, and a lot of the fauna that I come across is of the human species, which is often amusing and usually a rich source of anecdotes, and I suspect, a source that will never dry up. But today

I break with that practice and highlight an issue from a television programme. The programme was a couple of weeks ago but I've deliberately left it for that period of time, just to find out if I still felt as strongly about it. And I do. I think it's a perfect illustration of a lot of my messages about the need for balance in the countryside. It was a part of *Countryfile*. We were taken to some disused gravel workings near London. They were now flooded and provided several large areas of water that had been designated a nature reserve – so far so good. The programme features concentrated on the terns that live there. In order to enable the species to flourish, they were building some rafts that were to be anchored out on the water, the preferred nesting sites of terns to lay their eggs on. There was a small wire fence around each raft, about a foot high, to prevent predators like otters or mink climbing aboard and eating the eggs or killing the tern chicks. So far so good, sort of.

There was an island amongst these areas of water and on this island was a heronry. I think they said there were about 30 herons on it. We even went up a tree to see some heron chicks and saw them ringed before they fledged. Herons are clever resourceful birds, even cunning. So picture if you will, a heron waking up at first light on a nature reserve on some disused gravel pits. He or she will start the day a bit like you or me. It will have a bit of a stretch, a bit of a scratch, possibly a yawn or two and then it will think of breakfast. But it doesn't say to itself that it will have to scour the shoreline and shallow water for food. Because life has become much easier than that. Breakfast will be served conveniently on nice little rafts that will be identified by the herons as a food source just as easily as they identify the food source they have in fresh garden ponds that they soon empty of goldfish.

My brother made a nice pond that he stocked with expensive koi carp. Herons cleared it out in two weeks. The only unknown for the heron is if breakfast will consist of an egg or a chick. If it's a chick, it can't hide or escape because the raft has a nice little fence around it. It's all quite simple. If you want more terns you have to do something about the herons. Simple as that. If you make life easier for the herons, they will flourish to the detriment of all the species they feed on. For the heron, these rafts will be as welcoming and reliable a source of food as happy hour at a drive-through McDonalds except they won't have to pay.

***

The local wildlife group met in the pub the other night and after the meeting one of them told the farmers in the bar that they should all be forced to create about ten acres of habitat for lapwings. So I'll report it honestly. I'm going to walk the length of the room I'm presently in and look out of the window. We live in an elevated position and have superb views across our little valley. I'm there now. I can see two red kites, four carrion crows and a magpie. I will qualify that a little by saying that in the middle foreground is a pond and in that pond is a little island I created (about six feet across) and there is a Canada goose nesting there. Carrion crows, magpies, kites and buzzards are always hanging about in case she gets off the nest and they can get the eggs, so that could influence my little experiment. But I'm being up-front about that. Two years ago, kites drove the goose off her nest and ate her eggs. If kites can terrorise a large bird like a Canada goose off her nest, what chance does a lapwing have? The air around here is full of winged predators after things like breeding lapwings or skylarks or other ground-nesting birds. Never mind all the foxes and badgers that are about. Wildlife 'experts' abound in the pub, or on flooded gravel pits or on *Countryfile* itself, but when does naivety become stupidity?

25 APRIL 2015

I'm about halfway through my annual rolling of the farm. I roll all the silage fields, lest there should be stones lying on the surface that would get into the mower or harvester and I roll the winter barley.

It's a little bit later than usual but it's been a late spring. Most farm operations are carried out according to the season and the weather, not necessarily the date. I've left lots of nice dark and light stripes on the fields: the farm looks a bit like a veritable Wimbledon. The stripes have no effect on the benefits of the rolling but I know that my various landlords like them, because they have told me so. They think that they look nice, and if they think they look nice, that's fine by me.

I was a little anxious about the rolling this year. Rolling is a relatively slow job. I could do with a wider roller but there's no chance of that after six months of a milk price of 19½ pence per litre. Because it's slow, you spend quite a lot of time in each field and therefore have plenty of time to observe the wildlife.

My anxiety came from my concerns about the numbers of hares that would be left after the depredations of the gangs of poachers that have been about. After five fields I have only seen two hares, or was it one hare twice? You never really know.

Stephen is working ahead of me putting on fertiliser and he reports plenty of hares on the very top field of winter barley. More importantly, lots of hares and lots of tiny leverets. Nature is wonderful at rebuilding and fighting back, it's so resourceful.

I have one field that we re-seeded with new grass last autumn. The grass looks really well but it is accompanied by a mass of dead-nettles all in flower. I've never seen dead-nettles there before, so where did they come from? It's a bit like when they are digging out ground for major road works, the disturbed ground can suddenly be a mass of poppies, where there was no sight of a poppy before. The poppy seeds must have been dormant in the soil for decades.

There's another phenomenon associated with my rolling. When we are clearing out the chicken sheds during the winter, we put heaps of poultry manure out in each silage field that we will spread nearer the spring. We've spread all that a month ago but the heaps of manure will kill the grass beneath it and leave a bare patch. The bare patches are a bit unsightly so Stephen goes around and spreads some grass seeds on them before I get there with the roller, to press them into the ground. When I do arrive with the roller, each bare patch is a mass of small birds eating the grass seed. The one bare patch was in the middle of a 45 acre field, a long way from any hedge or wood, but the little birds were all there en masse. I suspect that the bare patches will remain thus.

★★★

Regeneration, that was the word I was looking for. Nature has a wonderful way of regenerating itself. And the best news I've heard lately is that the red squirrel population is up 7%. I had always believed that the reds had declined because the larger, more aggressive greys would steal their hoard of nuts. They may well do, but the real killer was the virus that the greys carry, which was wiping out the reds. But now the reds are acquiring an immunity to the virus and the population is on the move. That's not to say that we couldn't give them a bit of help. If you own a shotgun, have some grey squirrel shoots. Give them a hard time. Poison a few. Who knows, your grandchildren may be pointing out red squirrels to their grandchildren on a regular basis and telling them that they used to be rare. You aren't supposed to advocate stuff like that, are you? But doing or saying what I am supposed to do and say has never been my strong point.

★★★

A local retired farm worker has developed quite a nice little business catching other people's moles. At £5 a time, a successful catcher can accumulate quite a lot of money. Some mole catchers charge £10, I'm not sure why that should be: is it because they are less successful and therefore need more money? After all, a dead mole is a dead mole. And £5 is plenty. This man caught five on my son's lawn last spring, I should know, I paid him and I haven't had the £25 back yet.

But disaster has struck for the mole catcher. All of his traps were deployed in a lonely out-of-the-way churchyard, where the moles, to use mole-catcher parlance, were playing hell. Every single trap was stolen. A mole catcher bereft of his traps is a sorry sight. I've never seen anyone so disconsolate. In a rural community, if something is stolen, it is quite easy to fall into the trap (pun) of trying to identify the guilty party. And there was a ready suspect at hand. A local person who doesn't believe in death! So you have this vision of someone gathering up the mole traps because they don't believe in death, amongst the gravestones, where death is all about them! The traps were found a mile away behind a hedge, all broken! Which pushes our suspect a bit closer to the spotlight. It takes a bit of a struggle to follow the logic in this. It reminds me of the case where some badgers dug a large sett in a churchyard. There were bones everywhere but, because it was badgers, it was OK.

2 MAY 2015

Last week I was invited to North Somerset Young Farmers dinner and dance. I still can't get over how nice and welcoming everyone was to me. There's so much that's good, so much to admire, about young farmers and their clubs. It's all based on a philosophy of work hard and play hard, which is an excellent philosophy for life itself. If I have one regret about my own life it is that the path I had chosen, when I was of a young farmer's age, took me about the country a lot and I never had the chance to play a fuller part in the organisation.

It wasn't that good a day for me, I'd had a sore throat all week so my voice was not on full power and my knees decided to have one of their bad days as well, so I don't know what they thought of the state I'm in. Young farmers clubs raise prodigious amounts of money for charity and the caring side to their activities is much to be admired.

★★★

A couple or so years ago, a farming periodical did a survey of its readers asking which of the modern aids at their disposal had had the most positive impact on their lives. The mobile phone won by some distance. It is quite difficult to quantify just how useful the use of a mobile can be. For example, on Sunday mornings here, David would be here at home feeding cows their silage and I would go to the farm we rent to feed the young cattle. Calves can go through a stage in their growth, where if they wish, they can squeeze their way out of their yards through their feed barriers. So I could go to feed and one of the calves would be out.

I would then have this dilemma. If I left the calf out, it would soon find its way into the landlady's garden. But if I opened the gate to put it back into the yard, and it didn't go back inside in a seemly and cooperative manner (which sods law stipulates it won't), then I could have all the calves out, which quickly turns a mild inconvenience into a big job. So I give David a ring on my mobile and I go on with my feeding and he leaves his feeding and pops up in his truck and the calf is back in its shed and he is only delayed ten minutes and when the landlady gets back from church she hasn't got a garden full of calves.

The benefits are endless: get a puncture, get a breakdown, need some tea because you are working late, the list goes on and on. If someone else's plough breaks in half, in a distant field, everyone knows in half an hour. The problem is that the mobile signal around here has become crap. 'They' have shut a mast down to save costs. The power of the signal ebbs and flows like the tide. I don't really understand how it works. I can be sitting in my chair in the evening and the phone will beep and I've got several missed calls and they have all accumulated in the hour that I've been sitting in the same chair. I can get a text from someone a couple of miles away that takes five hours to get here! So where has it been? Has it got stuck in a cloud? Has it been sitting on a branch of a tree somewhere passing the time of day with some pigeons?

And there's a very serious downside to a poor signal. The combination of air ambulance and mobile phone has saved countless lives in rural areas. Road accidents, accidents in fields and forest, it's a modern facility, the benefits of which are difficult to quantify. A poor signal like ours has a massive downside, as we are about to see.

I've got some close friends who have a son of about 20. They don't have a farm but the dad has worked on farms all his life and the mum is a farmer's daughter, she also happens to be the florist I talk about. Well their lad loves farming and he's built up a flock of about 50 ewes and keeps some cattle in the summer. Anyway, he buys a second-hand bobcat on the internet. It could be that some of you don't know what a bobcat is: I think the correct definition is a skid steer loader. It's nothing like a polecat, which is a small furry animal that smells much worse. So he goes one evening to tinker with his new toy and come ten o'clock his mother says, 'I thought that boy would be back by now', so his dad goes to look for him, a mile away, and finds the loader has come down and trapped him and he's been trapped for three hours. His dad gets a jack and lifts the loader enough to free him. The boy could get to his phone but there was no signal. His father then had to leave him, drive a couple of hundred yards and stand on the roof of his truck to get a signal to dial 999. The boy had internal injuries that needed an operation. Like all young boys he is getting better fast, but it could have been so much worse.

9 May 2015

We don't keep sheep. We used to, but we don't any more. That's not strictly true, for two days last week I had 50 in one field. Yesterday I had about 20. There were different sheep scattered about in three fields. If you keep sheep you don't have much spring grass. If you don't keep sheep you usually have plenty of grass but other people's sheep want to share it with you. If other people's sheep comes into my fields, as they do, I leave the gate onto the road open. The owners of the sheep are more inclined to fetch them back if they get onto a road than if they are eating your grass. If they get onto the road they could end up in someone else's trailer and neither I or their owners will ever see them again.

***

It's General Election week and I have a very old story, but none the worse for that, it's old because it harks back to an era when people fixed things and things were made to be fixed. We had in our area an electrician who specialised in televisions: he had employees who did wiring and such like but televisions were his speciality. He had a nice little shop in our town and he had so many televisions in there in various stages of disrepair that he had to stack them outside on the pavement in order just to get into the shop. At the end of the day he had to complete the reverse procedure, put all the televisions back into the shop and shut the door. This scenario is so very different to that of today. Your television goes wrong and most times you are looking for a skip!

The procedure was that if your television went wrong, you would phone him up and he would come out quite promptly. I always remember that he always had a half-smoked cigarette that was unlit but somehow it was stuck to his bottom lip. Anyway, out he would come, and the back would come off your television and there would be much talk of valves and things that were a mystery to me. Most times he couldn't fix it, but not to worry. Outside your back door would be his estate car and that would be full of TVs. Some would be new and some would be second-hand. So he would go examining these TVs until he found one suitable to his needs. A bit like a golfer choosing a suitable club. And he would always find one that would 'keep you going'. And your faulty one would join the others in his car. It could well be that he left you a new one and you never saw yours again, unless it was on the pavement outside his shop. He would never send you a bill for the replacement TV. If you asked how much you owed him, he would say not to worry because he still had yours. Anyway, I've set the scene, here comes the story.

So he is in our house one day and he's got the back off our TV and I take him a cup of tea, and I watch fascinated as he manages to drink it without dislodging the cigarette from his lip and he says, 'I had an interesting incident last week'. A customer had phoned him and said he needs a new telly. So my man says, 'But yours is only three months old, I'll come out and fix it'. But the man insists that he needs a new telly. The conversation repeats itself back and forth, like a table tennis ball, and eventually the TV man gets out to the customer's house. The customer is sitting in his kitchen when he arrives and the first thing he says is, 'Where's my new telly?' 'In the car, but I'm going to try to fix yours first.' So he takes his toolbox into the sitting room and the television is sitting there on its little table and the screen is smashed. The man goes to have a closer look and inside the television, resting comfortably amongst the broken glass and destroyed valves is a gin bottle. The importance of the timing of this story is that this incident took place during the week of a General Election.

I never knew who the man was, my electrician was always very discreet, but you just have to admire him. Whatever his political convictions he had the strength of those convictions to put a bottle through the screen to switch the TV off. He was ahead of his time. There were no remote controls available. But if, over the past days you have reached for the remote to avoid a political message, does the mere pressing of a button do it for you? Wouldn't it be so much more satisfying to cast your opinion with a bottle through the screen?

16 May 2015

It's the last week of April and we have root crops to put in. The root crops are fodder beet and kale and they will provide winter feed for our cattle. It's quite a large percentage of our planned winter feed so it's critical that we get it right. About half will be grazed in situ by the cattle. In an average winter our dry cows and heifers thrive outside on these crops. It's a sort of 'green' solution to winter feeding: the cattle do the harvesting, their manure drops onto the ground where it will do most good. The cattle are off concrete which is good for their feet, and when the cold winds blow, there is warmth and shelter in the lee of the woods.

There's a downside. I'm always on about balance so I bring you the balance but it's also important to me to be honest with you. There's a small flock of lapwings on the field we are ploughing. I've been watching them carefully and I don't think they have started laying yet. The season is about two weeks late this year so I think we are OK. But the well-being of the lapwings and their nests is a large part of the urgency to get the job finished. The establishment of the crops is so critical to our winter feeding that I don't feel I have a choice. What I can do is provide the lapwings with choices. The next field is going to be fallow until July. It's an ideal place for lapwings to nest. There are good nesting sites in the footmarks of cattle. I think that what we are doing is working because last year we had five lapwings; this year we have 12.

So Stephen is adjusting his plough at the end of the field, just where the footpath runs, and he is approached by a walker. The walker tells him to stop ploughing the field because he is leading a walk across the field in three days time. Moving on quickly from that, the walker, who is belligerent, says we shouldn't be allowed to plough the field anyway because of the lapwings. This is a bit hurtful because we are already very conscious about this. He moves on, full of his own importance, and is followed 50 yards later by his wife. She stops to say hello and proves to be delightful, so 50 yards behind her husband seems to be a sensible distance. Stephen carries on with his ploughing and I go for a ride with him. With the two humans gone over the horizon, the wildlife returns. Following the ploughing and searching for food are 22 buzzards, three red kites, five herring gulls, countless carrion crows, one raven and a heron. If I were a lapwing I'd be more concerned about what that lot were up to than the activities of a sympathetic farmer.

★★★

The countryside can be a hard cruel place. A place of life and death. It can have its tragedies. It can be, and is, a far cry from the romantic notion that some people have of it. And sometimes it behoves me to bring to you the sad stories as well as the amusing, to bring to you a balance of what the countryside is really like. Today we have a sad turkey story. As we all know by now, my stag turkeys were getting out-of-hand. Very out-of-hand. Even though they now lived in a wood, they were a serious danger to anyone who passed by. They had also discovered how to get to the road and how to terrorise traffic. There was a very real prospect that they could have got on the road, that a lady would have got out of her car to shoo them out of the way and suffered serious injury. The stags weighed in at about 30lb each and all that combined weight, linked to all that aggression, was no joking matter.

So I enlisted the help of the keeper and we decided that two of the stags would have to go. He had mixed feelings about this. He thought it was very funny when they chased the 'guns' in the shooting season, but he didn't think it was quite so funny when he was on the receiving end himself. The scar that was inflicted on his head when one jumped on him out of a tree has healed up nicely and you can't see it when he has his cap on. But he still shows it to me every time we meet. I tell him to grow his hair longer.

He says he will shoot two of the stags. We decided to spare one to see if it will be less aggressive without two others to fight all day. And there's Christmas dinner to think of. There's still two hens to lay us eggs and possibly poults to rear. So he despatches two stags, he chooses which two, not that it would make much difference, they were all as nasty as each other. Next day he goes by the wood, just to see if it has made any difference to things, and the stag he left alive the day before, the stag that was a picture of health, the stag that was now able to enjoy the company of two hen turkeys, without having to fight for it, is dead on his back, unmarked but very dead. Just how sad is that? We went for tea to my daughter's last night. I chose to drive home by a circuitous route that I knew would take me past a farm where they also keep a few free-range turkeys. My wife, who is a main road sort of person, asks why I have come home this way, and I say I want to see if they have any spare stags anywhere. I can't repeat here what she said in reply.

23 MAY 2015

There's about seven of us sitting around the table in the pub and someone says he knows someone who is looking for two mudguards for a Fordson Major. Fordson Majors were built in the 1950s and 1960s so they are vintage tractors now. All of the company are interested in vintage tractors, three of them actually own various models. I don't own one, although the old tractor we use every day to scrape the concrete yards probably qualifies, but I'm the oldest here and these tractors were new when I drove them, so I am deferred to as a sort of expert.

Where I grew up, most of the farms in the area were small family farms about 50 to 80 acres, they mostly had one tractor and that tractor was a little grey Ferguson. The next tractors up the size scale were Fordson Majors. To tractor-mad boys, Fordson Majors were the stuff of dreams. Hardly anyone had a big enough farm to justify one. We only knew of one or two, but if we saw one, we were in awe of it, and even more in awe of the person driving it. I remember one day a group of us were waiting for the school bus when a new Fordson Major pulled up at the end of an adjacent lane and came out onto the main road and drove past us. Our conversation stopped dead, open mouths stayed open, we watched spellbound as the tractor went past us. The youth driving it seemed to look right through us as if we didn't exist. Yet two years previously he would have been standing with us to catch the same school bus! We were now a much lower form of life whereas he had moved onto life's pinnacle. We didn't feel slighted by this; it was just how things were. I noticed that the older girls in our group had stopped talking as well, they weren't interested in tractors, but they were clearly interested in the driver.

Years later I knew a man who owned two Fordson Majors, they were a lot older by now but not yet old enough to be vintage. One day he was driving one of the tractors down a farm track between two fields. He wasn't concentrating properly on what he was doing, I think he was trying to roll a cigarette at the time, he got one wheel up on the bank of the side on the track and the tractor flopped over on its side. It didn't flop right over because the sides of the lane were too steep, it just came to rest on an angle against a tree. He wasn't trapped underneath, the tractor didn't turn right over, it was leaning on the tree. But unfortunately the driver was pinned in place because his ear was trapped between the mudguard and the tree. (If you remember, Fordson Major mudguards was where all this started, I like my stories to go in circles, it saves me getting lost). He was pinned there by his ear for three hours before someone went looking for him. It was a simple matter for two men to push the tractor back over upright. It all seems quite funny now and I suppose that in a way it is, just as long as it wasn't your ear.

A few months later on a very wet day I took something to be repaired at the blacksmiths. It was a good place to go on a cold wet day, especially if he had the forge going. My man with the Fordson Major, and the ear, was there when I arrived and he was showing the blacksmith and me his damaged ear. Half of it was completely black and the considered medical opinion of myself and the blacksmith was that the black part was completely dead and needed to come off. I think they call it necrosis. To confirm our diagnosis the man with the damaged ear gets his penknife out and sticks it in the black bit and doesn't feel a thing.

We assumed, the blacksmith and I, that our man would go to hospital to have his ear tidied up, but a man who doesn't have time to stop a tractor to roll a cigarette, certainly doesn't have time to hang about in A and E. To our consternation and alarm he starts sawing away at the dead bit of his ear with his penknife. Either his penknife wasn't very sharp or he hit a bit of gristle, but he could only get halfway on his surgical journey. So the blacksmith finishes the job for him with the shears he uses for cutting sheet metal. He was not without his medical expertise, our blacksmith. There was a man in our village with only one leg. He had a false leg, a cumbersome affair made of tin, nothing like the modern prosthetics we see today. His false leg was always breaking so he had two, and one was always hanging up in the blacksmith's forge waiting for repairs. He had lost his leg in a tree-felling accident and legend had it that he was cutting a big branch of a beech tree but made the mistake of sitting on the branch he was sawing. I always thought this was a bit unfair because no one really knew it was true, and despite his disability, he was one of the hardest-working men I ever knew.

30 MAY 2015

I've got this friend. I've not seen him to talk to just lately, but whenever we do catch up with each other, the phrase he uses most often, when we are exchanging stories is, 'You cannot believe it.' I'm confident that that will be his reaction to the news that there are a group of people who seriously want to reintroduce the lynx to this country! It just beggars belief. It reminds me of a put-down Aneurin Bevan had for Harold McMillan, words to the effect, 'He says he is serious about this, and who knows, he might well be.' So why would you want to reintroduce an aggressive carnivore to a crowded island? An island that probably has ten million too many people on it. The lynx fan club is probably comprised of the same sort of people that are content to see our small bird and mammal populations decimated by winged predators. I have seen two articles in the national press lately that point out that birds of prey populations are getting out of hand. Perhaps the tide is turning at last. There is a supposed benefit to all this lynx stuff. The populations of deer are also apparently out of hand and the lynx will bring those populations back under control. Quite why it is OK for deer to be hunted but not foxes or badgers is also beyond my understanding. And how long do you think it would be, if you were a lynx, that it took you to discover that although deer were very tasty and provided a very good meal, sheep and calves, dogs and cats and children served the same purpose and were much easier to catch? About 24 hours I would guess. You just cannot believe it.

6 JUNE 2015

I know that I've reported on these phenomena before, but I still find it amazing. We've been getting our silage in and my job has been to rake up the grass into large rows before the machine that puts it onto the trailers picks it up. And as I drive around each new field, pied wagtails come out of the hedgerows to attack me. As I go around the field I successively invade their territories. It's quite remarkable, they hurl themselves towards the tractor. I've not seen one hit the tractor, but they come within an inch before they stop. They come so close that they disappear from view behind the tractor bonnet or the front wheels. You just have to admire their 'bottle'. How many times is their bodyweight less than that of the tractor, not to mention a 30-foot machine clattering away behind me? As my work proceeds and I move nearer the centre of the field, they stop attacking and watch me. Clearly they think that they have won the confrontation, and good luck to them.

★★★

Have you ever been to a farm sale? Everybody else goes. They turn up in their hundreds. These sales occur when a farmer is selling up and it is an opportunity for everyone for miles around to have nose. Farmers as a breed are nosey. They scrutinise every shed that they can get into, and quite a lot that they shouldn't. Many have no intention of buying anything, a lot will buy something if it's a bargain and some will go specifically to buy something. I've seen nearly-new equipment make more than new and about ten years ago I bought a corn drill for about £300, that I didn't need at the time, but I bought it because I thought it was worth about £1,500 (which it proved to be).

Most firms of auctioneers hold what they call collective sales of equipment on a regular basis. It is an opportunity for farmers and machinery dealers to dispense with stuff that they want to move on, and it is also an opportunity for some people to delve into the nettles around their yards and find bits of forgotten machinery that they throw some waste oil on, to make it look as if it works. Then they cart it off to one of these collective sales where it is usually sold to a scrap metal dealer, which is where it should have gone in the first place.

The most bizarre item I ever saw at one of these sales was a heap of wellington boots. They were all used, they were all colours, they were all shapes and sizes, there was a goodly pile of them, they were an indeterminate mix of left and right and there were about 50 of them. If you wear wellies on a regular basis it often occurs that a perfectly good boot can become damaged, sometimes you can repair the cut with superglue, if that fails you can put your foot in a plastic supermarket bag to keep it dry. But mostly you buy a new pair and keep the undamaged one of your previous pair, on one side, just in case it can make a pair up one day. But life never works like that does it? Next time a welly is damaged it's the same one and you end up with two or three left boots in reserve and one day they go into the wheely bin and that's the end of that.

But our welly story doesn't end there. Because I saw two or three people bidding for the pile of second-hand wellies, and afterwards the victors enthusiastically sorted them out. I think the pile made about £30. Both vendor and buyer had something in common, they were thrifty people, and thrifty is another word for mean. They were probably the sort of people who will always have more money than me. And what's the point in that? Because they will always be too mean to spend it.

The best farm sale story I ever heard was of a friend of mine who is a lorry driver. A lorry driver, maybe, but he came from a farming background and he loved spending any free time helping out on a farm of a friend he had. So the farmer tells him that the following week he is going to a very big farm sale he has seen advertised, a fair distance away. (In this instance, a fair distance is 150 miles.) And would he like to come for a ride? The lorry driver thinks this is a wonderful idea and he has a day off work so he can go. They get there in good time and watch each lot as it is sold in turn. Farm sales start with the smaller cheaper lots and progress slowly to the other end of the spectrum, usually finishing with tractors and combines. The lorry driver was more than a little surprised when the combine was sold to his companion. 'What the hell did you buy that for?' 'It was very, very cheap.' 'However will you get it home?' 'I thought you could drive it.' I don't know if you've ever been stuck behind a combine on the road, but 150 miles is a long way. Anyway, they set off and in the words of the lorry driver, 'He stopped at a garage every ten miles or so and bought me an ice cream to encourage me to keep going.' The mistake was not buying the combine an ice cream, because after 50 miles it burnt its belts out and they had to leave it at a farm and send a lorry for it.

13 JUNE 2015

Amongst the financial statistics that come out every month came the recent news that what was once inflation is now deflation, or to put it another way, inflation has become negative. Wise heads of commentators told us that this was OK, just as long as it didn't last too long. They said that a small negative for inflation combined with a small plus for income meant that most people were better off in the short term, so enjoy it. The present scenario is driven by lower fuel prices and lower cost of food. But is this 'short term issue' really OK? Because if you produce food, it's not. The pound is strong, other currencies are not, imported food is cheaper so the cost of all food is driven down. The demise of milk prices is already well chronicled, but beef, sheep and arable farmers are all moaning. Nothing new there, moaning is what farmers do. No one owes us a living so it's put up with it or shut up, because most consumers, our customers, clearly don't care about any bigger picture there may be.

The thing that intrigues me is that most farmers want to farm, but when what they are presently doing is no longer paying, they have, of necessity, to look at alternatives to try to make ends meet. It's called diversifying. It might be into solar panels, it might be into chicken sheds. But the objections to this sort of development are countless.

Through the window I can see a field where a farmer has put up about ten small sheds and runs, to rear partridge for a shoot. The sheds and runs combined are so small you could get one in our kitchen, but he's been reported for a breach of planning laws! Partridge only breed in the spring so he will only put one batch through the system, then the sheds will be taken down until next year.

At the other end of the scale I know of someone who wants to put up two large sheds for egg production. People miles away are protesting about noise and dust, issues that will never affect them because they are so far away. So my point is this: if no one cares if food producers are struggling, and they don't seem to care, and if they don't want them to do anything else, what do they want? I could sell all the grass and silage and fodder beet that I presently grow for my cows to produce milk, to a digester to produce power. We have decided, as a family, that if milk production is in the same bad way as it is now in two years' time, power production is what we will do. Lots of people don't like the concept of producing broiler chickens in large-scale intensive units. They dislike it so much, they would like the method banned. So I tell these people that there are 2.5 million of these chickens eaten in the UK every day. Then I ask them, if it was banned, 'What would you give them to eat instead?' I don't get an answer to that, because there isn't one. If UK farming is run down continually, what will you eat, where will your food come from?

20 JUNE 2015

Three or four weeks ago we were ploughing, working and sowing our root crops. You may also remember that I was told to desist these operations by someone who was organising walks over the footpath that crosses the land. That the same person, seeing that the argument about his walking activities was not going to prevail, pointed out the lapwings that were on the field and tried to use their presence to stop us ploughing as well. I resented that part of his argument because I was already very conscious about the lapwings and their possible nesting activities. Because the spring had been cold and late, I was fairly sure that they hadn't started laying yet. I think I'd got it right.

Last week we put some fertiliser on the root crops and I went for a ride on the tractor doing it. I've told you often enough that riding on a tractor gives you a privileged view of wildlife, that wildlife, to an extent, disregards tractors. Riding on a tractor, in effect, puts you in a mobile hide. And never before has that been better illustrated than that ride last week on the fertiliser spinner. The lapwings were still there, about ten pairs of them. They would let the tractor get within five or ten yards before they would move off. We counted 12 lapwing chicks and saw two nests with four eggs in each nest. That is what we saw, and I'm sure there were chicks and eggs that we didn't see. There were plenty of buzzards, kites and carrion crows about. How eggs and chicks had got that far is a mystery to me. I am told that lapwing chicks have to have drinkable water source nearby. This field is on the top of a high, dry hill so that is obviously a problem for them. We saw 15 leverets as well on the same field. Lapwings and leverets will not pay any bills but together that comprised a good day. The sort of good day that keeps you going.

★★★

I've got 'stuff' to do today so I've got up early to do this writing. It sort of suits me, it's a nice quiet time of day. Outside it's bright, sunny, but still cold at night for the time of year. It will very soon be the longest day! Then the days will slowly start to shorten. Before we know it, it will be Christmas!

There's a bit of a ritual to these early mornings. Put the kettle on. Open the kitchen door for the dog to come in. Our kitchen door is open all day long in the summer but the dog only comes in when there's just me about, because he's not supposed to be in our kitchen. He knows that only too well. He spends a lot of time during the day with his head just over the threshold but there's an unseen barrier, in the form of a sharp voice, that stops him going any further. Here he comes now, my dog, Mert. He's heard the kitchen door open and he gives me a good morning smile and settles down near my feet. Got a lot in common, Mert and I. We're both past our best, we're both getting old and we're both overweight. I think that's the end of the obvious similarities, because he's been castrated and, last time I looked, I hadn't.

But there's a bit of a ritual that I put Mert through every spring that really rejuvenates him. I take him to be clipped. I think that this year was his fourth year. The first year he didn't like it, he didn't liken it at all. He disliked it so much that we had to put a muzzle on him. The worst bit for him is the shampoo. Because he is a farm dog who lives outside, his coat is very dirty. He might look clean on the outside, but there's a lot of dust and dirt within his coat. So he has to have all that washed out or the clippers struggle. The lady who does it is very capable and pushes on regardless of the bared teeth that he is showing. They are not so much a grimace as the prelude to a bite. But once he's washed and blow-dried, his coat comes off quite easily. He gets a final spray with a doggy deodorant. I'm not sure he likes that either. He gets a lot of sniffing from David's dog when he gets home. He looks and smells so different that this other dog wants to fight him!

The transformation in Mert's demeanour is quite remarkable. The amount of hair removed is huge. At a stroke he becomes more comfortable and more active. In effect it takes years off him. I just wish a haircut would do the same for me. But then, my haircut costs £4.90, Mert's was £30. I suppose you get what you pay for.

27 June 2015

We used to have a bad habit (well, we have several, I'm just focusing on this particular one). If a filing cabinet became full, we just bought another one. The first filing cabinet we ever bought is in the kitchen, full of 'stuff', but we never use it. We've got two more in the 'office', that are also full so I thought I'd go through the one in the kitchen and do a bit of clearing out. The trouble with this sort of clearing out is that it takes longer to read what you have found than it takes to put it into a wheely bin. I found some articles that I'd written 15 years ago. One article concentrated on a cut I had sustained in some new wellies. I had told how I tried to mend the cut three times with superglue, that I'd failed and that I had had to resort to putting my foot in a supermarket bag before I put the welly on, to keep my foot dry. The purpose of the story was to say that money was tight, that I'd got to make the best I could of the ruined wellies.

So here I am, 15 years later, and I'm still short of money. Everything in life is relative and relatively speaking, things are as difficult now as they have ever been in 50 years of dairy farming. But me and my wellies, with a cut in them, do not constitute hard facts. Deep down in the drawer I find those hard facts. There's piles of old dairy costings. I find that in April 1997 I was getting 23.89 pence for a litre of milk. Today I am getting a headline price of 24.1. I'm fairly sure that 1997 is 18 years ago! Off hand, I can't remember any riots about the price of milk. So people must have been able to pay whatever it was in the shops. The irony is that I am one of the lucky ones. There's lots of dairy farmers getting less than I am. Some are getting down towards 16p.

★★★

I continue to trawl the newspaper and internet in my search for a corgi. A corgi that I can afford. So in the course of my search I come across all sorts of doggy adverts. There's a dog rescue centre not far from here that has recently been looking for homes for two sheepdogs. They are old dogs, ten and 11, they need to find homes together, and have in the past, so we are told, been successful at sheepdog trials. The advert tells you quite a lot more than that. It tells you that they were dogs that were good at their work: why else would they live to that age and stay on a farm? It's a logical conclusion: farmers with a lot of sheep need good dogs to tend them. If the dog's no good, they get or breed another.

But these two weren't just any old sheepdogs, they were good enough to be taken off the farm, to trials, open to public scrutiny. Those are the things that the advert tells me. Those two dogs lived long, useful, productive lives on a farm. And their reward? They are dumped at a dog rescue centre. What sort of person/or farmer, would do that? I must admit that if we didn't already have two working dogs, I'd have been down there. I've never ever been involved in dog trial work although over the years I have had some really good dogs. (I've had plenty of the other sort as well.) The really good dogs were so intelligent that they knew your fields and pens so well that they already understood what you wanted to do with your sheep and instinctively went on and did it.

I once had a bearded collie that was called Poppy (a stupid name for a working dog but she already had it) and she was probably the best dog of all. She slept on the yard just outside the kitchen window, rain, cold, snow. She would fetch the cows every morning, unbidden, when she heard me get into the kitchen and put the kettle on. I bred a son out of her that I called Bill, he had a better name than his mother, but he was just stupid. He used to spend his days barking at the birds sitting on the electric wires. I had the pick of the litter and he was useless!

People who bought other pups out of the same litter would phone up and say what good workers they were. Just shows what a good judge of a pup I am! Bill was no trouble but I'd bought a collie that would work and Bill would get beaten up, quite regularly, by the collie and the corgi we had at the time. The milk tanker driver found him a home in a town. He gets stroked every day by the children going to school and he goes on holiday to the Lake District twice a year. There's a happy ending for you. Some dogs have terrible lives. I knew of a dog that spent its life chained to a diesel tank, so no one could nick the diesel. But then keeping an active breed of dog shut in a small flat on its own all day is probably just as bad.

4 JULY 2015

It's two or three years now since our late blacksmith's shop was converted to a home. I drive past it most days but it still seems strange to see it as it is now and to remember it as it was. Fifty years ago it was a local meeting place, a hub of the community. Because if you were engaged in something in the fields with a machine and that machine broke, off you invariably went to have it fixed at the blacksmiths. And when you arrived there you could be in a queue of other farmers or their workmen who were in a similar predicament. That made it a sort of social gathering, because everybody joined in to help with the repairing, and soon you were at the front of the queue.

But there was a downside to this. If you needed your machine to be fixed that day, for example, harvest machinery, a half hour job could last three hours because of the queue system. As farms became more mechanised and employed fewer men, there was a gradual urgency creeping into farm life. Farmers would no longer countenance their men being at the blacksmiths for half a day and started to buy electric welders of their own. And that was the start of the 'finish'. It was probably inevitable really, but it was also a shame. Because there was as important social side to life which finished as well. And there used to be some fun.

A great practical joker was our blacksmith. Like the apron he wore, his hands must have been made of leather. His favourite trick was to give you a piece of really hot metal. 'Just hold this a minute'. Because he was holding it in his hand, you would assume that it was OK in yours. Many a time I've seen him give someone something hot to hold and the metal in question would go clattering to the floor and the victim would be dancing about nursing a burnt hand.

If there was one thing that hastened his demise it was the fact that he had such small premises. It was a small stone-built building. The first room had a stout wooden floor, presumably because it was better for horses to grip at shoeing time. The next, smaller room, was where the forge and bellows were. Apparently this area was so special it had to be incorporated into the new home as a condition of the planning permission. But there was nowhere that you could park a tractor and implement in the dry whilst you repaired it. I'm not really sure how an electric welder works but I do know that there's a lot of electricity involved. Not big on electricity me: if I have to get past an electric fence I get down on my belly and crawl under it. Holding a piece of metal whilst it was being welded back into place, in the pouring rain, was not for me. Many a time I've felt a bit of a tingle coming through, that shouldn't have really been there!

He needed a two or three bay building in addition to what was already there, where tractors and implements could pull into the dry. He had the room for it because he had some land around his house and buildings and he used to milk a few cows as well. I've milked his cows for him a few times while he fixed something. Now I look back, I always had to pay him to fix the machine but he never paid me for milking his cows! Not that it mattered over much, that's how things used to work in those days.

I always remember a piece of homespun philosophy he gave me. He said that you should never go off for the day unless it was too far to come back to do the milking. I suspect that needs some explaining. In the many years that I did most of the milking, the very thought that you had to be back at home in good time to do the milking in the afternoon would easily spoil your day out. Much easier therefore, not to go out in the first place. Which is what I did for 20 or 30 years and what explains the blacksmith's advice. It was OK to go off a really long way because it then became worth getting someone in to do the milking for you. I'm sure that lots of people who milk cows regularly will understand this.

★★★

Yesterday I went to our local 'town' to fetch the Sunday papers. There's a few people standing about, clearly waiting for something. Some are wearing hi-vis jackets and looking very important, as they usually do. A town crier comes around the corner and announces that it is the day of the midsummer rejoicing and down the street comes a procession. It is led by three lots of morris dancers, well two of the teams are ladies so I'm not sure what they call them. And there's a cart decorated with rushes and finally the clergy, including what looks like a bishop. They are on their way to the bottom of the town to a church service. I don't really understand it all, I thought that the summer solstice was to do with Druids and paganism. Seems a bit of a mixture of cultures to me. My daughter later explains that it's also to do with John the Baptist. Anyway, Mert my dog enjoyed the procession. I notice that when they get to the bottom of the town, most of the dancers give the church a body swerve and go into the pub.

11 JULY 2015

I went on a train journey yesterday. Haven't been on a train for a long time. I always find it fascinating. I look closely at every field and can usually remember it in detail. So on the return journey I can remember the shape of the field, and I can say to myself, 'I think this is the field with the black bullocks in' and sure enough, there they are, at the other end, under the trees. I saw two fields of linseed, a crop I've not seen for some time. Some years ago it was quite common but now it has largely disappeared. If I remember rightly, those that grew it reckoned it was the very devil to get through a combine, but if you picked just the right day it would combine just fine: the trouble, apparently, was knowing exactly which was just the right day. It's a pity that it is rarely grown now because when it is in flower it is the most beautiful blue imaginable. It's such a beautiful blue that if I were an artist and was painting a landscape, I would use my artistic licence to put in a couple of fields of linseed, even when they didn't exist, just to show that lovely blue.

But I'm not an artist. My brother and sister are both accomplished artists so they had all the artistic genes that were available in our family. I had to make do with all the brains, good looks and personality.

And then the train comes to a town. I always think that it's a bit intrusive, going through a town on a train. It's as if you are seeing the back of everything, the back as if you have lifted someone's shirt tail up and had a look at their backside. You see into the gardens that back onto the railway line. Some gardens are an oasis of colour and tranquillity, where people have made a real effort to create something that is nice. But next-door's garden might be a tip, full of the detritus of modern life. What always strikes me, at a time when there is such a great need for new housing (a need that puts pressure on the need for green belt development), is just how many brown field sites there are within our towns. These sites are largely cleared and presumably waiting for the right commercial opportunity. But they could be made so nice for housing. Dirty, heavy industry is largely gone these days. Some trees and grass could make them lovely places to live. Putting houses there would tick a lot of boxes. Save farmland, be closer to work, tidy up the view from the train. It's such an obvious solution to a very real need. A need that apparently took a second place to greed. Nothing new there.

18 July 2015

Today I use one sentence, quite deliberately, that I have used before, 'Anything that you feed to a cow to produce milk can be put into a digester to produce electricity.' To enlarge on that, what I am saying is that farmers grow crops to feed their animals. But they also have choices now about what to do with those crops. And if the profitability of putting animal feed into producing power is in excess of putting that same feed into an animal, slowly but surely, that is what will happen.

This year we have grown 50 acres of winter barley. We grow it as a cash crop, a crop we can sell. That means, conventionally, we could combine harvest the barley at the end of July and sell it as soon as we could. There would be a by-product to this, the winter barley straw that we would bale. Winter barley straw is very palatable and can be fed to cattle.

So it's quite easy to work out what the crop will yield in terms of grain and straw, less the cost of the contractor doing the combining. The only negative would be if the weather proved to be wet and you had to have the grain dried. We don't have a grain drier so we would have to find someone to dry it, cart it there, and cart it back. It's an expensive scenario, one that you don't like to think about.

So there we have it, 125 tons or so of barley that will end up as animal feed somewhere and some nice barley straw that we can feed. But there's something else we have as well. We have this nice young lad turn up on the yard. He is of a farming family I know of who live 20 miles away. He says he's heard we have 50 acres of winter barley and would we like to sell it for his digester? So we take him to see it and he offers a price that is in excess of the calculation we have if we take the conventional route.

He does all the harvesting, we lose the straw but we don't have the cost of combining and the possible cost of drying the grain. Within a week he's taking it. He's carrying it away with 11 tractors and trailers. When they are queued up at the start, it's like a wagon train scene from *How the West was Won*. It was a good deal for us, it was a plus, a plus that buoyed us up.

But not for long, because next day our milk price went down another penny. Which for us is a bigger negative than the plus we had for the barley. The barley fields are next to the 40 acres of fodder beet we are growing. The lad says 'I'll buy all that as well'. Who is to say that he won't get it? These farm digesters are going up everywhere, there's 40 gone up in the next county. If you want to drive change, the best and quickest way is to drive it with money. That's the driver behind solar panels and wind power. Whether it's a good thing to drive power production at the expense of food production remains to be seen. I've spent my working life producing food so this doesn't sit that comfortably, but my bank manager would say it is a no-brainer.

★★★

I keep remembering stories about the blacksmith. I was there one day, when his father was still alive, in his 80s but he could still shoe a horse. They'd fallen out because the father had booked a horse in to have its feet trimmed. There wasn't much room there to work, so the son had had to move all his welding gear outside in the rain so that they could bring the horse inside. I was inside as well, preferring the chance of being kicked by the horse to being electrocuted outside where the younger blacksmith was welding metal in the rain.

There was a teenage girl that had brought the horse. It wasn't shod but was out at grass and had been brought to have its feet tidied up. So I ended up holding the horse's head while the old man busied himself with the feet. A great practical joker was the old man.

He was removing hoof exactly where it needed removing but each time he would stand back and look at the horse's top-line as if what he was actually doing was trimming the feet in order to keep the horse level.

The girl was about 14 or 15, and she watched all this going on with eyes that grew wider and wider. He was in his element and milked the situation for all it was worth. Eventually he eyed the horse up and said he thought it was about right.

So he told the girl to hold the horse so that I could check as well. I was enjoying all this, so I got a long spirit level, put it on the horse's back, and said that I thought it was still a bit high on one corner. He had a look too, 'I think you are right'. So he took the merest sliver of hoof off one foot. Checked the spirit level again and pronounced the horse good to go. I don't know who the girl was. Never saw her again either.

25 JULY 2015

Yesterday I was taking the cultivator through the stubbles left when we removed our winter barley crop. I was breaking them up so that we can harrow them and put in some stubble turnips that we will let for winter sheep keep. As my work progressed over the field I saw ten hares make their way, quietly, to other fields. There were lots of birds examining the newly-disturbed soil for worms and grubs. Mostly they were rooks, a few pigeons and a pair of red kites. Kites have now worked out that it's the action of the cultivator that finds them food. The one kite was flying along within two or three yards of the tractor and at a lower level than the cab floor, sometimes it was so close I felt I could reach out to touch it. It was slightly in front of me, presumably it hadn't worked out yet that the best pickings were to be had just behind the tractor. Seagulls worked this out lifetimes ago.

It was a very windy day, blustery. I always imagine that air moves about very much like water, but you can't see it. It's only when there is a medium about that the wind can carry, like dust, for example, or some very dry hay, that you will see more spectacular whirlwinds. Yet the kite navigated its way through this gusty wind with hardly a movement of its wings. It was almost as if it was finding holes in the wind and was using them for its safe passage. It was an excellent opportunity to study a spectacular bird close at hand. In due course, hindsight will surely tell us that there are too many of them about.

★★★

You may remember that earlier this year we had a dilemma when we had to cultivate a field for root crops at the same time that a small flock of lapwings seemed to have settled on the same ground. The dilemma comes from the fact that we have to go ahead with establishing our root crop, we have to be able to feed our cattle next winter. At the same time, the lapwings had clearly chosen a part of the same field as a possible nest site, and we very much wanted them to be successful as well. I had a hunch at the time that both lapwings and I would be OK, because the spring had been cold and I didn't think that they had started laying.

About a month later we went over the same ground with some fertiliser and saw 12 lapwing chicks and eight eggs in two nests. We were so delighted that everything had worked out well.

We told all our farmer friends and they were as pleased as we were.

Despite the popular perception, most farmers spend their lives amongst wildlife and love to see it flourish. Since then that field has been a strictly no-go area for us. Our aim was that the lapwings were to be left undisturbed so that they could successfully rear their young. From a distance we could see that the adults were still there, flying about.

It's a big field, 45 acres: we have an area of fodder beet where the lapwings are, then a 15 acre patch of ryegrass and then more fodder beet. There's a footpath crosses the bottom patch and I'm out looking at how the crop is progressing when two walkers come over the stile. We say our 'Good mornings' but they don't carry on along the footpath, they set off up the field. I gently point out to them that the footpath carries straight on. 'We know that, but we can see lapwings flying about so we thought we would go up and see them.' I tell them that they have chicks up there and they are clearly delighted. 'Ooh it will be lovely to see them.' I explain that in my humble opinion the birds are best left undisturbed and that they shouldn't go. They don't like it, in fact they make it quite clear they resent it. They get back on the footpath and continue on their way. I get the clear impression that they will be back, at a time that I won't be there to redirect them. It's strange that I end up being the bad guy in all this.

★★★

If you are a farmer and you do a bit of writing, it is inevitable that you will score spectacular own-goals, by testing providence. In the spring I told you about the tendency of some of my neighbours to share their sheep with me. This was based on the simple principle that if you have sheep in the spring you are always short of grass. If your neighbour doesn't have sheep, like me for example, he has plenty of grass that your sheep will spend 24 hours a day trying to get to it. But it's a spring phenomenon, or it usually is! We have a field on the outside of our block. We took a crop of first-cut silage off it, put some fertiliser on, shut the gate and left it. It's alongside the road but we have let the hedges grow up to two metres (supposed to be better for wildlife, but I have my doubts) so you can't see into it. Soon it's time for second-cut silage and we take the mower in there, we fire it up, it's quite noisy, and all these white heads pop up out of the long grass, like U-boat periscopes. There were about 50 ewes and lambs in there!

8 AUGUST 2015

Some friends of mine have a local friend who hand-paints crockery and they came upon one of her hand-painted milk jugs [see p.190]. They were so taken with it that they bought it and sent it to me. I'm quite taken with it as well. It is painted in the manner of a pastoral scene and within this scene are ten clearly live and healthy badgers and two up-ended dead cows. I know that the majority of you reading this will find what I have described distasteful.

I also know that most farmers reading this, who have cattle, would think, like me, that the milk jug is very appropriate. That's not to say that any of us are anti-badger, it's just that the TB issue is beginning to grind us down. We are used to adversity, if you deal with livestock and the weather on a daily basis, adversity comes thick and fast. That in itself is a part of being a farmer that you enjoy, in a sort of perverse and masochistic way. But in all other issues we have, we can always see an end game, a light at the end of the tunnel.

There is nothing at all going on at the moment with the challenge of bovine TB that shows that sort of light. There's absolutely nothing going on that even shows where the tunnel is. There are acres being written about it but very little going on. Plenty of discussion on whether to cull badgers or not but none of the action, which was actually promised.

There's just as much discussion about the vaccination of badgers against TB. This is the 'silver bullet' that many people pin their hopes on. I can understand this because it's a benign solution. But it shouldn't necessarily be compared with a bullet. If a cull is the answer, there are more humane solutions than shooting. But a vaccination policy would be deeply flawed. By its very nature it is random. It relies on catching badgers, and no one really knows what percentage of badgers have been caught and therefore vaccinated. Experience shows that the same badgers are caught on a regular basis and that the obvious conclusion of that is that some badgers are never caught.

Science has proved that the best time, the most effective time, to vaccinate a badger is at seven or eight weeks old. A time when your badger cub is living well down its hole. The private consensus of vets is that badgers constitute 25% of the bovine TB problem. It's a percentage that cannot be ignored, because if you ignore a percentage of that scale you will never ever get to the light at the end of the tunnel.

So where are things now? Well, I know a dairy farmer who is trapped into one of the lowest milk prices that are being paid. He is locked in there because no other milk buyers are recruiting. So to keep his cashflow as near to positive as he can he has been selling his close calving heifers. Now he's gone down with TB so that avenue of income is closed to him.

We've just had our annual test. A week before we had our results, a farm a few miles away had 25 cows identified as TB reactors and they have gone for slaughter. We passed our TB test but please try to imagine just how agonising that week of waiting was for our results. I sent a text to our bank manager, I was so pleased and surprised. If we had failed and could no longer sell our beef cross calves I honestly don't know what would have happened to our family business.

We've got quite a large garden and we try to keep it nice for our bed and breakfast guests. It's not that difficult because the views from the garden are superb, so people tend to look at the view and not the garden. I'm not much of a gardener but I do keep the lawns looking nice. Badgers have had three goes at establishing a sett in the middle of one lawn. Each time they have made a hole about two feet deep. Each time I have taken a spade and put the soil off the lawn back down the hole. This is illegal. Just how crazy is that? I show my new milk jug to everyone who calls here. Its pictorial message is as eloquent as anything I could write.

★★★

I was at a hog roast last night. It was OK, but the crackling wasn't much. So we are sitting there eating, and this pig is lying in the carving tray, about five yards away, staring at us, trying to make us feel guilty. And the conversation turns to pigs. My companion tells me the story of a cottager who had a pig in the sty in the garden. And he tells a friend that the pig looks OK, but it isn't growing much. So the friend comes to have a look and decides that the pig, a Large White, is not growing because it's lonely. 'I've got some Gloucester Old Spots,' he says, 'I'll bring one across and put it with yours to keep it company.'

Next day he sneaks into his friend's garden with a paintbrush and some black paint and puts some spots on the Large White. He hides the evidence and then goes to tell his friend that he's brought a pig across. The two go down the garden to see how the two pigs are getting on. Of course there is only one pig there. 'Oh dear, my Gloucester Old Spot has eaten your pig!' It was the only conclusion. 'Never mind, you can pay me for my pig, as and when you can afford it.' And the owner of the pigsty believed this for about three weeks, until the black spots started to fade.

15 AUGUST 2015

At this time of year we have a fair drove of dry cows and in-calf heifers out at grass. They need plenty of scrutiny and attention because it is in summer that they can get what we call summer mastitis or what used to be called August bag. This problem is caused by flies and can result in a very nasty mastitis that is difficult to treat, invariably resulting in the loss of the quarter of the udder affected and if not quickly detected, can result in death. But when you are going slowly amongst these cattle, on full alert, with your eyes peeled, you see other things as well. In the last week I have come upon the corpses of five leverets. Still quite small, perhaps two or three weeks old. They carry the clear signs of death by badger. Different predators have different ways of killing. Your fox will always take the head off. A badger always attacks the rib cage. Many years ago we had a badger killing lambs: the lambs' rib cages were always opened as neatly as if they were cut with secateurs so the badger could eat the vital organs. All the leverets had their rib cages opened up in a similar fashion.

***

Talk in the pub lately has been of silage-making. Most grass around here goes into silage clamps, especially on dairy farms. Beef and sheep farmers mostly make their fodder into large round bales. They prefer to make round bales of hay because then they wouldn't have to buy plastic wrap. But we've had a lot of showery weather so hay-making has been very difficult and most of this fodder has been wrapped in plastic. Most land around here is sloping, so when a bale is dropped by the baler it has to be dropped across the slope or it will run away. If this is not done with care there are interesting stories of bales making a dash for freedom. It can build up quite a speed, your runaway bale, which can be quite funny if it's someone else's bale and you are being told about it in the pub, but not so funny if it leaps a hedge and lands on your Saab convertible!

We have had a tractor and rake fully committed to a local contractor's silage gang this season, it's a way of trying to bring in more money, so we've had plenty of stories on that score. I think these self-propelled forage harvesters are just amazing. They look, for those of you who don't know, a bit like a short version of a combine harvester. The cut grass is raked up into rows, 30 feet of grass going onto one row, and the harvester gobbles it all up at a great speed, cuts it into lengths of just a few centimetres (notice how easily I slip between metric and imperial measures) and blows it all into trailers running alongside. It takes huge horsepower and a drum of very sharp knives to do all this. So the last thing you need is something entering the mechanism along with the grass, that shouldn't be there.

The obvious thing to avoid is metal. There is always the danger of picking up a bit of metal, it could be a very old horseshoe or a piece off your muckspreader: whatever it is you don't want it in there. So all these 'choppers' are fitted with metal detectors. These will stop the pick-up mechanism dead in its tracks if there is some metal amongst the grass. It will find a bit of wire as big as a clipping off your big toe but it will sometimes let a plough share through. The resulting noise and damage can be spectacular. Stones are another problem. There are stone traps designed to collect stones, that to be fair, sometimes work. If a stone gets through, the damage is dependent on the nature of the stone. Some stones will shatter and all you need to do is sharpen the knives. Some stones are made of sterner stuff, will get badly bruised, but will do as much damage as a piece of metal.

But time and the seasons move on and people have been getting their combines out of their winter sheds and getting them ready. The combines for their part have been standing out on yards waiting for the weather to come right, ready to go, as if they were flexing their muscles. The weather came right yesterday afternoon and, as if at some signal, I could see three combines start into winter barley at two o'clock. These modern combines have huge cutter bars and are taking a lot of corn in at a pass.

So the story reaches the pub of a new combine making its way tentatively round its first field. Suddenly there is a terrible noise from the drum mechanism followed by a progressive rattle through the machine. It was clearly a serious noise, but not a terminal sort of noise! A bit like a nasty cough, and with a few more coughs, it will clear itself. So the driver stops the combine but leaves the mechanism running and he can hear the rattle progressing through the machine. He goes to the back where the straw comes out. The rattle stops and a bike drops out onto the straw. As yet there is no confirmation as to whether the bike was being ridden at the time.

22 August 2015

I spent a couple of hours with an old friend of mine recently. I've known him a long time now and he's well into his nineties. He doesn't live that far away and I really should pop around to see him more often. He's not that mobile but he gets to his local pub for a game of dominoes two or three times a week. The pub is right on the side of the road and the car park is the other side of the road. So he sits in his truck in the car park until someone spots him sitting there and they pop across, get his zimmer frame out of the boot and see him safely across the road. And the procedure is repeated when it's time to go. We were both reminiscing, which was almost inevitable.

Many years ago we both rented land off the same landlord. He was a really good landlord and every year he would invite his tenants for a day's shooting, the week before Christmas. It was something we all enjoyed and looked forward to. We'd all go to the pub mid-afternoon and have a Christmas dinner, have a good time and the day would last well into the night. None of us should have driven home, but most of us did. It was something we did in those days, a mile down a narrow lane was deemed as OK. Most of us had done a bit of rough shooting but the tenants' shoot wasn't rough: the landlord organised it just as he did on one of his proper shoot days with his syndicate. He had beaters and everything, which was a real treat for all of us.

I need to explain, for those of you who don't know, that at the start of a proper shooting day, all the 'guns' draw a number out of a little wallet that decides which peg you will stand on at each drive and you move up, say, two pegs at each drive. So if there are eight pegs, the best places to stand are in the middle of the drive, say number four. But on the second drive you will be number six and the drive after that number eight. This system is devised so that in theory, everyone gets his fair share of the good shooting. But there are a lot of narrow valleys around here, so that the middle numbers might be in the middle of the valley floor but number one and eight, which were at the ends of the line, would have a steep climb to get to their position. Which brings me back to the friend that I went to visit.

There was him and another farmer who weren't that good on their feet but I was young and fit. So at each drive one of them would sidle up to me and say 'What number are you this time, Roger?' And I might say that I was number four. Then they would say 'I'm number eight but I'll never be able to walk up that bank, can I go at four and you climb up to number eight for me?' Which I would do, I didn't mind, it was a good day out and it didn't really matter. But then it did. Because the landlord was bustling about to make sure everything went smoothly for his guests.

And he had his work cut out. He was a bit like a sheepdog trying to get a small flock of sheep in the right place. So I would be standing at number eight and he would come out of a wood or through a gate and say 'What number are you, Roger?' And I would say number eight, and he would say that I was OK. Then he'd think about it a bit, and he'd say, 'But what number were you on the last drive?' And I would say two. And there'd be a sort of exasperated noise and he'd say, 'But you should be down there on number four now, I thought that adding two to your number each time would be simple enough: how you added two and two and got eight is beyond me.' 'It's too late now, the beaters have started, just remember you'll be six next drive.' And off he would splutter. He clearly thought that I was one of the thickest. I never told him why I was on the wrong peg. But at the next drive I could very well be one or two or seven or eight according to the terrain and my friend's stamina and the landlord would poke his head over a hedge, look at me, shake his head in disbelief and wander off again.

29 August 2015

There was recently an article in our daily paper about how much of our food we waste in the UK. The figure they quoted was way ahead of anything that was wasted in the countries of our European neighbours. It was a top of the league position we should be ashamed of. There is absolutely no doubt that food supply in this country is taken for granted. People think that food comes out of supermarkets but it doesn't, it comes out of fields, and they fail to make the connection. Why value a piece of cheese for example if you bought the one piece and the retailer gave you another piece, just the same, for nothing? So if you don't eat all the second piece, so what? It didn't cost anything. And then there's all these crazy eat-by dates. Every breakfast time I trawl the fridge and eat all the food that has gone past its time. I'm still OK. Sort of.

There have been important anniversaries of the end of the Second World War and we've had an insight into what rationing was like. I can still remember us as a family having one egg apiece a week, and what a treat it was to have that egg for Sunday breakfast! As a family we were allowed ¼lb of sweets a week and my Dad would send me to the shop to fetch them on Saturday afternoons. We would have a family discussion about what sweets we would have and when I got home he would weigh them again to make sure I hadn't eaten one! I had a man who worked for me 50 years ago who had been a shepherd in the 1920s and 30s. He often told me that if he was having a difficult lambing and he thought the ewe would die, he would hasten her demise with his knife and take her shoulder off and take it home for the family to eat. I think that this shoulder of mutton was so important to the family's diet that he was quite flexible in the judgement made as to the ewe's chances of living. Most people will find the idea of eating the shoulder of a dying ewe appalling but I bet that there are millions of people in the world today who wouldn't hesitate to do the same. So we waste all this food, apparently over 300lb of it per person, per year and the beneficiaries are urban foxes and seagulls that continue to proliferate. On a personal note, a farmer note, it's clearly not easy producing food for a population who take that food for granted, and undervalue it.

★★★

I didn't know whether to believe this story or not. What credibility it has comes from the farmer who told it to me. He's a really nice, level-headed sort of chap, not much given to frivolity and nonsense, like some farmers I know (me for example!). He tells me that two engineers are putting a cable in past his farm and the cable has to be buried as it goes past a gateway. They come across the yard to him, indicate the mini digger he has parked there, and ask him if he'd mind just cutting a five-yard trench out for them. He doesn't mind at all and the job is soon done. The farmer indicates what he has done, asks if it is OK, and suggests that they just tidy up some loose soil and a few clods that still lie in the bottom of the trench. They agree with him and ask if they can borrow a shovel to do the work.

The farmer expresses surprise that they have with them two vans, both full of equipment, yet do not have a shovel. They explain to him that somewhere or other an engineer hurt his back doing a bit of shovelling and received some serious amount of money in compensation. It was therefore decided that all the engineers had got to go on a 'shovelling course'! But in the meantime, and until they had completed the course, all shovels had been confiscated. The farmer found this a bit hard to believe so they took him to the vans and inside there were these painted sort of stencils in the shape of each item of equipment and where it should hang on the inside of the van. In each van there was the painted shape of a shovel, that was empty. What do you think? I think it has a hi-vis, fluorescent yellow, health and safety ring of truth about it.

12 SEPTEMBER 2015

We were talking about milk prices in the pub and then the conversation moved on to discuss how many farms in the immediate local area had ceased milk production since the demise of the Milk Marketing Board, which was in the 1990s. We got up to about 16, all within six miles! Once a farm goes out of milk production it is almost unknown for it to return. It seemed a natural progression for the conversation to go on to discussing churn milk collection. Today, all milk is stored in refrigerated tanks whilst it waits to be collected. Looking back to churns, it's a wonder how we ever kept it marketable in hot weather. I once worked for a man who would put a couple of teaspoons of a chlorine liquid into each churn of the evening milking on hot thundery nights in August, to stop it going sour. This was clearly illegal, yet it is still OK for water companies to put exactly the same thing in water supplies to keep them safe. Seems a bit of a double standard.

But there's still a churn story to come. There was a small farm that milked about 20 cows that had quite a long farm track to the main road to take the churns down to the churn stand. Most farms had churn stands on the main road, a sort of raised deck that was the same height as the bed of the lorry that collected them. You can still see many of them today although they haven't been used for years and years. If he was at home, the farmer's son would take the churns to meet the lorry in the farm van after morning milking. It was always a close-run thing, getting the milk down the lane in time to catch the lorry. And if the milk wasn't there the lorry would not wait but go on to the next farm. There was no alternative but to chase after the lorry in the hope that they would catch it up somewhere. The farmer's son would always put his dad's cap on if he had to drive on the main road. He looked a lot like his dad and he thought that if he met someone who knew him on that three-mile drive to the next farm, that they would think it was his dad if he wore his cap. After all, he was only twelve.

19 SEPTEMBER 2015

I went to hospital last week for some tests. I'm not going to tell you what the tests were for, I have to keep a shred of privacy, all I'm going to say is that the tests made my eyes water, and it was nothing to do with my eyes! What I am going to talk about is driving. There was a time in my life when I had to drive about 30,000 miles a year but these days I drive a small fraction of that. I have two vehicles, both quite old. I have a 4x4 to go around the farm in, because my mobility is not that good these days. And I have a car that I use if I have to go further afield. So I went for the hospital appointment in my car and my daughter came with me and she reckons that if I had to take my driving test again, I would fail it on roundabouts.

We're driving home, well I'm driving, and we come to a very busy roundabout, and I decide I will make a special effort to get the driving right. There's three lanes going in and we are to take the 3rd exit so I take the outside lane and after two exits I move into the middle one so I can get out into my exit which is a dual carriageway. I do all this, and think that I have done it all quite well. Apparently not, because I get some very loud horn blowing from behind me. I ask my daughter what I had done wrong and she says that I have done nothing wrong at all (which is a bit of a surprise). The car behind gives me a couple more blasts and then overtakes me on the inside and I get one of those hand gestures that apparently means 'have a nice day'. But after about 200 yards, the car turns off down a road that goes nowhere else but to a retail park. And I'm reflecting that it's a bit sad if you get impatient to just go shopping. As he turns off I give him a couple of blasts of my horn, to get my own back, and I can see, by the way his head is moving about as he tries to work out who is blowing a horn at him, that I have really wound him up. He hadn't wound me up at all so I put it all down as a personal victory.

There is a lesson that can be learnt in all this, and the lesson is all to do with farm trucks. I rarely go more than ten miles from home in my truck. More than ten miles and I usually take the car. But there are certain advantages to using a truck, especially in heavy traffic. My truck is high mileage but quite reliable. And it shows what it is and how it earns its living. It's very well scratched. Its scratches vary from the sort you get from the caress of a briar, through to the deeper scratch you get from a thorn bush, to the more serious scratch of barbed wire. It's very well bruised. Bruises on trucks are usually called dents. It gets dented for example when you drive fast through a muddy gateway, in the hope that your momentum will carry you through. You often lose the ability to steer with these manoeuvres but the gatepost will usually guide you through. The important point of all this is that if you are driving a well-scratched and dented vehicle in heavy traffic, and it clearly doesn't bother you if you acquire some more dents and scratches, then you get a lot of respect from other road users. You can change lanes on roundabouts as you like, no need to give signals, gaps open up for you. I'd like to drive my truck through the London rush hour, just to see what would happen, but it seems too much effort.

★★★

I've got a friend who has a truck a bit like mine. Last week he was going around the sheep on his top fields. He has a steep farm with a lot of fields above the house and yard, what we call a 'sharp' farm around here. Anyway he has driven around the sheep and is preparing to drive home and he needs to open the gate to get out of the field he is in. He parks a short distance from the gate across the slope, because, as he later says, 'the handbrake doesn't always work'. As he is opening the gate he hears this sort of rattling and squeaking noise, so he says to himself, 'That's the sort of noise our truck makes'. And he was right, because his truck was off home without him. It went about half a mile down this steep hill and in doing so crossed two grass fields and a field of oats. It went through three hedges, though to be fair it nearly cleared the one. At the last hedge it took out a thorn tree that was surely 12ft thick. It came to rest in a duck pond. Thirty yards to the right, it would have hit a bungalow. Ever the optimist, he thought it didn't look too bad and he had a mechanic to have a look at it. But his truck is a bit like mine, it was only worth about £500 before it went through those hedges. All the cables and pipes that are fixed to it underneath, well, it left all them behind. Very sadly the mechanic described its injuries as terminal. He's looking around for a replacement and he's got friends, people like me, for example, asking if he wants one with a handbrake!

26 SEPTEMBER 2015

My son reports seeing a hedgehog on the yard. He reports it because he reckons that he hasn't seen a live hedgehog for more than ten years. He's always about very early in the mornings to do his milking and reckons that years ago he would see hedgehogs every day, especially when he was down the fields fetching the cows for morning milking. We 'real' country people are in no doubt that the reduction in the hedgehog population is directly linked to the expansion of the badger population. But what do we know? I can never work it all out. It's OK for cattle and hedgehogs to reach an untimely end but not a badger. We all laugh at pictures of cows in India, grazing with impunity on market stalls. Yet we've allowed the badger to achieve sacred cow status in this country.

★★★

'They' were talking about other people in the pub last night. They were going back through the family tree of a particular family with a sort of accuracy that would be the envy of one of those websites dedicated to that purpose. They get back about four generations to an old granddad. 'He died in the hay field.' Of course that requires further explanation. It seems that the family had a big field of hay all baled up in those small traditional bales that you rarely see these days. It was really good hay but rain was forecast before morning, the sort of heavy rain that could spoil hay. All the family were out to lend a hand except an old granddad who had a bad heart.

But as the clouds started to gather, he could contain himself no longer and he went out to lend a hand. It was all hand labour getting these bales in and it was taking a toll on the old man. They completed a load and as it went off to the yard and they prepared to start on the next empty trailer, he quickly counted the bales still left out. He said, 'There's two full loads left here and there'll be a couple of layers of bales on the last trailer. I think I'm going to die and if I do you can put me on top of the bales on the last load and take me home on that.'

And that's what happened. He did die and they put him on top of the bales on the last load and took him home. And they got all the bales in before it rained, so there's a sort of happy ending as well.

3 OCTOBER 2015

Yesterday I went for a ride around the farm to check on our root crops. They are all doing quite well in the showery weather but challengers in the form of flies or slugs can come along, as if from nowhere, and wreak havoc. I'm reading a novel about wolves in America at the moment, where they call animals that they consider a nuisance varmints. Slugs and flies would fit comfortably into that category. All is well with the root crops and as I drive out I take a diversion across 25 acres of winter barley stubble. A stubble, especially one that is off the beaten track, is a good place for a hare to lie up for the day and I went to see if there are any about. There aren't any, well none that I disturb anyway, but at the far end there are about 30 lapwings. I assume that these are the same bunch that have been about since the spring, they have bred up here and seem quite settled. We must be doing something right.

★★★

Last week we had a 3-day break. We went to Devon. Specifically we went to stay on the edge of Exmoor. Very taken with Exmoor, me. I never tire of criss-crossing it. I'm seriously thinking of buying a farm on Exmoor and if I get a big lottery win, that's what I will do. A girl who worked in the pub where we were staying was telling me that, come the autumn fairs, there would be plenty of Exmoor ponies available at £1 apiece. Can't quite see the point in breeding them. Why not turn out mares and fillies and gelded males? When the animals become of little value the chances of neglect increase. A sad fact, but true.

★★★

People's drinking habits are interesting. Although I go to the pub two or three times a week, I don't think I have a drinking habit. I don't go to the pub in order to drink, I couldn't drink much anyway as I have to drive home but mostly I have two glasses of wine. I go to the pub for the company of the people I know I will meet there. I hardly ever drink at home. I've got drink here and if you called and it was an appropriate time of day I would offer you a drink and have a drink with you but off-hand, I can't remember the last time I had a drink here.

There seem to be two clear distinctions of pub trade. Most pubs around here are quite busy at around five o'clock. The people there at that time seem to fall into the category of those who are 'having one on the way home,' which can mean two or three or several. This phenomenon seems to be particularly prevalent in builders around here. The only variation to this habit, with builders, occurs on Friday afternoons when the pubs are full of builders from two o'clock onwards. I've always thought that being a builder must be a very rewarding profession, because most of the builders I know seem to pack up work for Christmas at the end of the first week of December and sort of filter back towards the end of January.

Anyway, the early evening trade in pubs seems to drift away by eight o'clock and the sort of second sitting starts at nine o'clock until late. Nine o'clock is the time I go and when my friends all go. To be honest it would suit me if we all went a bit earlier, because going at nine o'clock usually means I don't get home until 11.30 and I like to get up early but most of my friends have work to do in the evenings after they've had their tea. But the early evening drinkers include several people who work really hard all day, who will work seven days a week if it is required of them, but the five o'clock visit to the pub becomes an essential in their lives. Several times I have heard farmers say to me, 'We've had so-and-so helping us this week, he's really good, he'll shift a lot of work, the only trouble is he gets a bit restless by about half past four and he's always gone by half past five.'

A farmer I know was telling me that he had a contractor baling some straw recently. 'Boy, he can shift some bales; the bales were coming out like machine gun bullets. He did the field in no time at all and he was finished by half past four. When I went for the evening paper, the baler was in the pub car park. He always liked his drink. When he was 13 years old his mother had to bribe him to go to school. She had to give him enough money to buy a pint and he would slip out of school at lunchtimes for it.' Just what sort of school allowed him the freedom to do that? Never mind what sort of pub served him every day?

10 OCTOBER 2015

We did our third-cut silage two or three weeks ago. Because our silage clamps were all full, we baled the grass into large round bales wrapped in plastic. The moment these bales are wrapped, no harm can come to them. (Except, perhaps when the multitude of pheasants are pecking holes in the plastic!) But we've been a little tardy in picking the bales up. When we did it was very interesting to travel, by tractor, onto various fields to see what was going on with the wildlife. There are hosts of pheasants. I've told you before about cock pheasants being aggressive in the spring but I've never seen if before in the autumn, so every move by the tractor and trailer was followed by about ten cock pheasants who wanted to fight you! The flock of lapwings is still with us, so that's a success story, but there's surely twice as many skylarks about as there were in the spring.

And then there are the hares. With corn harvest done everywhere and lots of clear fields, here come the hare coursers again. This year there are six men and 11 dogs. We saw a couple of mutilated hare carcases that were the work of dogs, no doubt there were more. We saw a lot of leverets, they were still smaller than rabbits, and would have little chance against all those dogs. Fortunately, the police are showing more interest this year. Their advice is to keep well away and to avoid confrontation. Coursing makes me so angry that I don't know if I could, were I to come across it. There's a very wise old adage that says 'Use your head for thinking and your feet for dancing and running away'. Seems sage advice in these circumstances.

I've even tried to analyse why it makes me so angry. Hunting doesn't make me angry. I didn't come from a farming family. My first attempt at farming was to keep hens at the bottom of our garden and their eggs provided my pocket money. Then I used to rear twelve cockerels for the Christmas market every year: they provided a lump of money of lottery-winning proportions. One year in early December, a fox killed the lot. It didn't eat one, just killed them. Any foxy sympathy I had went out of the window. I'm not anti fox hunting because I don't like people who live in towns telling people in the countryside how to live their lives.

I haven't seen a badger for years but I know they are about because I see their tracks and their setts. They don't bother me as long as they don't have TB. If they do, they should be treated the same as cattle. Simple as that. I don't think I could put up much of a fight against six hare coursers, probably never could. But if I came across them I would be tempted to block their vehicles in a field with my truck whilst I hid behind a bush and phoned the police. The hare is such an inoffensive animal.

★★★

We've not had a lot of field mushrooms this year. It soon went too cold at nights as the autumn approached. And when we do get some, they are shared out with friends and family. I always take some for my landlady which she always appreciates. But I suspect that the biggest problem we have is that there is only one place where we find any, and there is a public footpath running right through it. So we are probably sharing the mushrooms with a lot of people we don't know as well. Many years ago we used to get a lot of those very big horse mushrooms, just one would fill a frying pan on its own, and I would have one for tea every night, as did the young lad who worked for me at the time (good job we had two frying pans). We had one a day each for weeks until one night we both thought we were about to die. I've never eaten one since. But there's a lot of people around here eat puff balls. They rave over them. They apparently slice them up, peel the skin off, and fry them. Then they go into raptures over them, mostly in the pub. So, because I hadn't had many mushrooms this year, I was tempted to try a slice of puff ball. Very bland, I thought. Not worth any risk there might be.

17 OCTOBER 2015

I don't think that there is a collective noun for pheasants [Ed: Roger, if you had our book *A Murmuration of Starlings*, £7.99, you'd know that it's a 'nye'.] But there is probably a noun that I can borrow that serves the purpose. The one that comes most readily to mind is pack. This is the time of year when there are pheasants everywhere. They have grown beyond recognition in the last month. They have grown in size and their plumage has grown. They've not yet had the rude awakening that will soon come when they discover that their sole purpose in life is to be shot at.

But at present they enjoy life to the full and are roaming about in large packs. They travel long distances, to the despair of keepers, who are trying to keep them at 'home', lest they stray onto other shoots and don't come back. I'm sure that there are a lot more pheasants on my land than last year but the keeper reckons it's the same number. So why did he need to erect an extra rearing pen and why are there a lot more feeders about if it's the same number? I'm not quite as dull as I look, which is very fortunate.

So these packs of pheasants roam about the fields, eating insects that they catch and spilt grain where they can find it. They are browsing their way about a bit like a grazing herd or flock might. But I was on the tractor the other day, on the top fields and near the boundary, and I could see a large group of about fifty pheasants in the next field, a field that is on the next-door estate. They were busying themselves, much as I have described and their activity took them closer and closer to the hedge. One popped through into my field and in no time at all they were all through.

But their collective behaviour changed immediately. They weren't foraging for food, they were all on full alert, their necks stretched high as they would go. What it told me was that they knew, or they certainly appeared to know, that they were on a field where they shouldn't be. Suddenly, as if at some signal, but not one that I could detect, they raced back to where they had come from, where they returned to feeding as if nothing untoward had happened.

★★★

I was writing at the kitchen table last week with the door open and, on a sort of daily cue, my poultry flock turn up. There's a cockerel and six hens. First they inspect the dog's bowl for any fragments there may be and then they make a tour of the kitchen. They don't do it if my wife is about but they seem to know that I don't mind. It's something I love, this small free-range poultry unit. We mostly find where they lay and they've been providing plenty of brown eggs. They won't come today because the fox has had them all. I could replace them and I could keep their replacements in a hen house and run. But that's not what I want to do. As for the fox, he or she is only doing what foxes do, I just wish it would do it somewhere else.

★★★

We have just had the most beautiful week, weather wise. Lovely misty mornings followed by warm sunny days. We've been getting a field ready for winter barley. It's so lovely ploughing up there on early mornings, up there in the sun, and down below, the mist in the valleys. It minded me of an incident many years ago when I had a young lad working for me. He was keen to get back to ploughing and in an attempt to wind him up I told him that you should never plough mist in. Warming to my theme, I told him that if you plough the mist in it stays there under the furrow, all winter, cold and damp and it would be so cold and damp that it would affect the growth of the new crop.

Becoming ever more eloquent, I told him that sunshine was a very different matter. It was a good thing to plough sunshine in. Cupping my hands together, to illustrate my point, I said that if you ploughed a nice little ball of sunshine in, it would shine beneath the soil all winter, bringing warmth to the new plant and helping to sustain it until the spring. But there was another employee listening to my little story. A much older man. He had listened to the concept of sunshine shining beneath the soil all winter with fascination. 'Well, I've worked on farms all my life, and I never knew that.' The fact that he had believed what I said quite made my day. To the extent that misty mornings and ploughing still remind me of it.

24 OCTOBER 2015

I'm up on our very highest field. It's been ploughed and I am working the ground down with the power harrow. Further up the field, covering the ground that I've already done, comes the tractor and drill, planting winter barley, next year's crop. The seed drill fits best on 'my' tractor, so I am on our newest biggest tractor, which is a bit of a treat. It's a bright sunny day and it's quite warm in the cab, although I know that outside there is a cool wind blowing. I could adjust the temperature controls to have a perfect working environment but I'm not sure how to work all the buttons, which is also true of the other controls on this tractor.

The only temperature control I'm really sure of is shedding clothes. I've already taken my fleece off and next time I get to the end of the field, off comes the pullover. So far it's not a good day for bird watching. From where I am I can see for miles in all directions and there are tractors busy everywhere, so the birds are spoilt for choice of where to go for food.

Most of the tractors are like us, they are planting next year's corn crops, but I can see two gangs busy getting up potatoes. Out of nowhere comes a large flock of rooks and they are busy feeding on grubs all over the field. Then just as quickly they are gone but not to worry, over the hedge come 'my' flock of lapwings. This is the field where they mostly seem to live: rather them than me in the winter.

The local wildlife group have heard there's lapwings about and have been trying to find out where. Those of us who know won't tell them, which really miffs them, but it is they that told the world, via social media, about my hares, and we all know what happened to them.

The lapwings settle right where I am working and as I approach they just shuffle apart so that I pass right amongst them. Next to join us is a solitary buzzard, it looks as if it is this year's hatch and it seems to be finding plenty of food.

But not for long, because here comes a red kite and that soon moves the buzzard on. The kite tries to bully the lapwings but they only move a few yards away and don't seem too bothered. As I go back and forth at my work, both kite and lapwings are within five yards or so of my tractor and I get the chance to study them so very closely. Two more kites turn up and three bullying kites are too much for the lapwings and they eventually move down to the other end of the field.

It's nearly dusk when we are finished and the dark hills have tractor lights working everywhere late into the night. I go up to the field next day to retrieve some equipment and it's nice to see the field well worked and drilled, all nice and smooth.

But that's not all I can see. It wasn't just tractor lights that were busy in the fields last night. Because the nice smooth field has got the footprints on it of about five men and several dogs. I can track them right across the field to where they climb over the fence into a neighbour's field. So that's my day spoilt before it's started. Hare coursers are nothing but persistent. The next day after that I go up to roll the field. I don't usually roll winter corn in, as the frost usually break the soil down further during the winter, but this field has worked up a bit 'fluffy', and needs firming down. The hare coursers footprints are all over the field and there's enough footprints to make me suspect that they came two nights on the trot. Which is further bad news. Logic tells me that they wouldn't have come back unless they had found some hares to kill.

I do a lot of this tracking; I'm doing it all the time almost subconsciously. I can tell different people's tyre marks in gateways and if it's marks that I don't recognise I try to follow them to see where they went and what they were up to. I fantasise about finding the hare courser's vehicles parked out of sight somewhere when I am on my loader tractor. I'd pick one up and put it in a ditch and put the other on the roof of it. We know the make and colour of their vehicles and the police know their numbers, but still they come. If I come across a car parked somewhere secluded and the windows are steamed up I leave it alone, no harm in that, not that I know of.

31 OCTOBER 2015

It's the keeper on the phone. What does he want now? He's very animated. It's his first shoot next Wednesday but it's not that. It's the hare coursers he's concerned about. It seems that they are now coming two or three times a week. Yesterday, on his rounds feeding the pheasants, he picked up five mangled hare bodies, but it's very difficult to catch them at it. How do you arrest someone for taking a dog for a walk down a lane? The perpetrators know all this full well and are very brazen when confronted. Some of them have come 80 to 100 miles so they are not going to be put off that easily. The police reckon that adjacent police authorities have more officers that are dedicated to wildlife crime and their activities have pushed the perpetrators into our area. They emphasise that we should not get involved in any confrontation, 'There is so much money changing hands, they won't care about anything that happens to you'. The coursers are not far from other crime. The keeper managed to get the registration number of one four-wheel drive. Turns out it belonged to a Transit van that was scrapped five years ago.

★★★

I went to a neighbour's funeral the other day. He was a farmer and he had died at 90 so it wasn't that sort of really sad funeral. It turns out that not one night in all those 90 years had been spent away from the farm, apart that is, the few weeks he had spent in hospital at the end. Most people will find that amazing. That he'd never even been on holiday. Yet the person who gave the eloquent eulogy told the life story of a man who had lived life to the full. A man who was a real character, a life story full of amusing adventures, a life full of fun. And in our lives, the lives that most people live, isn't that a heartening story? In a society that seems driven by a celebrity culture and material possessions, that there are people who live full and happy lives within their community? And he's not a lone example.

Years ago a good friend asked me to take him to Carlisle to buy a bull. He asked me because he hadn't a clue where Carlisle was. (Round here I'm considered to be widely-travelled.) That night in Carlisle was his first time away for 20 years and I don't think he's been away since. I know of a farmer a few miles away who has only been 25 miles from home once in his life, and that was as an outpatient at the hospital. I quite like the idea that although there are people who devote their lives to filling our newspapers with adverts for cruises, for example, there exists a small sector of society for whom those adverts go right over their heads.

7 NOVEMBER 2015

We've had a bit of a family crisis since I last wrote. I'm not about to give free publicity to an organisation that certainly doesn't need it, so all I will say is that there's a plastic thing that lies on the floor underneath our television. Well, that packed in. Bringing out a replacement took five days. So for five days we didn't have television. Well it was three days really, because after three days it started working again, occasionally, but we didn't tell the man who brought the replacement that.

It shouldn't have been the issue it was because there are three televisions in our house. There's a small one in the kitchen, there's another in the B&B guest room. But it's a lot to do with where you sit when you relax and where you are comfortable sitting. And in front of our main TV is where we are comfortable sitting. It's a bit like an old dog getting into his dog basket and going round and round to flatten down imaginary grass or whatever, it's what he does, it's what he is comfortable doing.

It wasn't so bad for me, I had one of those odd weeks when there was something that I had to go to every night, after several weeks when there was nothing in the diary. But after three days the missus was quite grumpy. So in due course the man turns up and puts a new plastic thing under the telly and you could be forgiven for thinking that order was restored.

Not a bit of it. We go very quickly from crisis to anarchy. In his misguided benevolence not only does he leave the plastic thingy, he gives us a new remote control device. And he leaves the old remote one. Which is still working perfectly well. There's nothing, well very little anyway, more annoying than someone who keeps flitting from one channel to the other, all the while putting CEEFAX on to see if there is any rugby news. This is what I do, I do it all evening. I look at other channels while the adverts are on. Now there are two of us doing it. I'm not sure that anarchy quite describes what is going on. I can't see, if there is to be an end to all this, quite where that end will come from. Because when we are not watching TV we both hide our respective remotes so that the other can't find it. I suppose that, inevitably, the batteries in the remotes will go flat, but that will only be a temporary solution.

★★★

Yesterday, Saturday morning, we were moving some cattle from one field to the other on the road. We had a grandson to help us. After we had finished I took the opportunity to have a ride around the fields. How are the turnips growing? What's the fodder beet like? Is the winter barley up yet? That sort of stuff. I was particularly looking out for hares as well.

For the first time for ten years I didn't see one. Well not a live one anyway. I saw the body of one that had been ripped apart by dogs. That's not to say that there weren't any, there could well be, but because they are being terrorised by coursers on a regular basis, any remaining hares are probably now very shy and keeping their heads well down. The keeper has his first shoot this week so the beaters may have a better idea of how many hares are still about. There's 40 acres of fodder beet and about 20 acres of turnips still there, so I'm hoping that that is providing sanctuary for the hares and that it's difficult for dogs to hunt through as these dogs hunt by sight. And there's lots of woods to provide cover as well. The young daughter of a neighbour has been looking for her cat for a week now. It's a cat that was often out in the adjacent fields. I don't expect coursers' dogs differentiate between hares or pets. It's all sport to them.

14 NOVEMBER 2015

It's 8.30 on a Sunday evening, I've just got changed to go to the pub. The keeper is on the phone. 'Your dry cows and in-calf heifers are all out on the road.' I grab a torch and a grandson and go to investigate. The keeper was out with a couple of friends lamping foxes so he'd come on these cattle before they had gone too far. By the time I arrive he's got them back in but not all into the right field. The cattle have got out because someone has quite deliberately opened the gate to let them out. There's been a spate of this around here lately, cattle let out onto the road and always dairy cattle. It's not for me to point the finger of blame, but in one case, where the farm buildings were on the side of the road, the farmer's dairy was ransacked and slogans daubed on the wall that said, 'Milking cows is cruel'. There's no need for me to point fingers because this is a vegan calling card and they were pointing fingers at themselves. It's the sort of thing they write all the time in their endless letters to the press.

I've no problem with other people's points of view, I can understand where vegans are coming from, but why is it so important for them to impose their views on everyone else, in this case with illegal activity? There were 45 cattle in that bunch, mostly black: what do they think will happen to them, out on narrow lanes in the dark? In a worst case scenario, people in cars could get injured as well as the cattle. In the very worst case scenario someone could get killed and someone else could be looking at a manslaughter charge.

★★★

I'm going to see my daughter. It's a beautiful sunny day and I'm in no rush, so I go the 'back' way, which is via five or six miles of single track lanes through beautiful countryside. Actually what I'm doing is taking her what you read. I still write it all in longhand and she types it up. I do it in longhand for two reasons. It's what I'm comfortable doing, I haven't got to worry about any technical issues pertaining to a keyboard, doing it in longhand seems to make my writing flow better. I do emails every day, but I've never progressed beyond using one finger. It takes a very long time. Occasionally my laptop seems to get bored with it all, so I might have been working for an hour or so, and suddenly the screen will go blank. I'm a bit self-taught in all this so try as I may I can't retrieve what I've just written and I usually have to wait for a passing grandchild to do it for me, which they do, so successfully and quickly, that I never get a chance to see how they do it.

Anyway, I'm driving along these narrow country lanes and I come across the pink and black-clad form of a young lady jogger. Except that she isn't actually jogging, she's standing in the middle of the lane with her back to me. As I'm in no rush, I sort of coast along until I'm right up to her. I stop about ten yards away and see that she has earpieces in her ears and she is fully concentrated on what I assume to be a mobile phone and she looks as if she is texting. She's still not aware that I am there and I allow the car to ease forward until I'm so close that if she fell over backwards she would be sitting on the bonnet. Still she doesn't know I'm there and continues to push buttons on her phone.

The longer this goes on the more amused I become. There's the car engine going and I've got the radio on. Still I sit there and the radio goes through two more records, so what's that, another five minutes? The longer this went on, a blast on the horn seemed less and less appropriate. Suddenly she plunges her phone into a top pocket and carries on jogging. I follow at about ten yards behind her. She still doesn't know that I'm there but after about 200 yards she does look back over her shoulder, sees me and pulls to the side! I pull alongside her and wind the window down. 'That must have been a very important text you were sending.' She tells me it wasn't a text, that she was having trouble locating the music she wanted to listen to. 'How long were you there?' she asked. 'About ten minutes.' She was a bit embarrassed about that, but only a bit. Narrow lanes, blind corners, I would have thought that being able to hear traffic approaching or coming up behind you was fairly important. We get a lot of people hurtling around these lanes on mountain bikes; they've often got earpieces fitted as well.

21 NOVEMBER 2015

My dog Mert is getting to be a very old dog now and doesn't go far. I don't know how old he is because he was an adult when he was given to me. He can't jump into the truck any more and so we don't go on adventures together. He spends most of his time sleeping in the place where our heating boiler lives. He comes out at regular intervals to bark at the wind and the moon and if these excursions should coincide with the arrival of someone at the back door he still frightens the life out of them. Sadly I don't expect him to survive the winter.

There's this old Granddad died up in the hills. He was in his late 90s and hadn't been ill, so there's no need to upset yourself about it. His relations phone a friend of mine who does outside catering and ask her to do the refreshments after the funeral. She asks when the funeral is to be. 'A week on Saturday.' She says she's sorry but she's already booked to go away for the weekend. 'What about Friday, then?' She says she's already got a funeral to do on the Friday. 'What about the following Monday?' She says yes, she can do that. 'That's when we'll have it then, I'll tell the funeral director.' Nothing like having your priorities in a proper order.

5 DECEMBER 2015

When I was driving on a busy dual carriageway a couple of months ago, traffic cones sent us into single file. This single file went on for miles and miles. The reason was that they were cutting the grass either side of the crash barrier in the middle of the road. So that's OK, but what struck me was the fact that the grass each side of the barrier was just as wide as the tractor that was doing the cutting. So if the grass was two meters wide each side of the barrier and you multiply that by several miles, you have a considerable acreage (or hectarage, according to your age), that could have and should have been sown down to a wild flower seed mix when the road was constructed. What a missed opportunity! There's millions of acres like this around the country if you include the vast areas of grass on the sides of busy roads and motorways. There are plenty of voices in the media telling farmers that they should be growing this sort of wild flower meadow, but I've yet to see anyone advocating using the sides of roads. It's always an easy shot, to have a go at farmers because they are a minority. It feels like, 'don't do what I do, do what I say'.

★★★

Some years ago a field that adjoined a local town was up for building development. It was bought as a whole by an organisation that sought to establish an eco-friendly, commune is not the right word, houses for like-minded people is probably a better description. I've nothing against that, it's just that it's not for me. The concept was that only a part of the field should be developed. That the houses should not have large gardens but that there would be allotments to grow vegetables. And that a fair proportion of the land was left to its own devices so that it reverted to scrub, spinney and eventually woodland, woodland that they could all share. But, and there's always a but, these aspirations meant that in order to achieve all these possibly laudable aims, the houses had to be built very close together, most people think too close, in fact at first glance it could be called a ghetto. And these are not cheap houses. You can buy some really lovely houses around here for that sort of money. When they were built, a proportion of them were supposed to be affordable, which implies to me that they are meant to be priced within the financial scope of people on the lower rungs of the property ladder. Some chance. Ideals and ideas are all very well, but in the end practicalities will out. Because the houses are expensive and large and because the plots they have built on are small and close together, the houses tend to be high. Window cleaners have been reporting for some time that they can't clean the windows because the houses are so close together that they can't get an angle on their ladders that make them safe to use. The ultimate and final, very final, practicality comes from our wise undertaker: 'The stairs are so narrow and so steep, you just can't get a coffin down them.' I didn't ask him how he managed, I'd rather not know.

12 December 2015

Everyone's trying to reduce demand at hospital A & Es. It seems simple to me. You charge everyone who goes there £5. Unless they are drunk, if they are drunk they should pay £50. You could easily decide if they had had too much to drink by breathalysing them. £5 is a bit tough on the genuine needy but it would weed out the time wasters. And it would be worth the £5 because if the time wasters weren't there, they'd get much better treatment.

I'm not anti-drinking. Many years ago I was at a rugby club whose base was at a pub on the upper floor of an old outbuilding. To get to the club room you had to negotiate a very steep, narrow, high staircase. Well, you know how it is. One thing leads to another. It was a day or so before Christmas and when I went to go home, I missed a step and went headlong to the bottom! The time I took to descend those stairs is a record I still hold to this day. Looking back at the incident, I'm not sure if I got knocked out as I fell or if I just went to sleep when I got to the bottom. Whatever, I was asleep/unconscious long enough for them to call an ambulance. I was a lot more aware of what was going on by this stage and it has always been a disappointment to me that the driver who took me to hospital, didn't put the blue light on.

I wasn't in hospital long but when they discharged me they gave me a piece of paper that said 'fell downstairs, drunk'. I've still got the paper somewhere, but not seen it for ages. I'm not proud of it, neither am I ashamed. It's just one more escapade in the passage of your life. But there was a cost to the NHS for my escapade, and I should have paid it.

19 DECEMBER 2015

For some time now I have had to adhere to a strict management regime for my hedges. It has been a part of my stewardship agreement. This has meant that lots of hedges are only cut every other year and those that aren't are allowed to grow to two metres in height. When I had the plan originally it was so complicated, with different bits of hedge in the same field due for different treatments, that to do it as first envisaged would have meant being with the contractor all the time he was there (three or four days), so I've sort of simplified it now, don't know if I should have but that's where we are. It means that the answer comes out the same, it's just that I've devised a different way of getting there.

The other odd thing is that I don't really know why 'they' want these taller hedges. So I make assumptions. If a hedge is two metres high, you end up with twice as much hedge as you do if it's only a metre high. Presumably the powers that dictate this sort of stuff think that to be a good thing. And if a hedge is only cut every other year, presumably any food growing on that hedge stays there until it's eaten. Or am I presuming too much?

What I have noticed, however, is that hedges that are two metres high and hedges that are cut every other year, are altogether looser hedges than those that are cut every year. And it is quite easy to imagine how that would happen. Hedges that are cut every year are much thicker, more impregnable. And that is the key word here.

One of the most distressing sights that I see every year is the plundering of fledglings, as they leave their nests, by predators. When small birds fledge they spend a few days in the hedge in the vicinity of their nests, while they find their feet, or in this case their wings. At this stage they are vulnerable to predation by magpies, carrion crows and buzzards. If the hedge is dense and thorny, these birds cannot get within the hedge to seize their prey.

The two metre, cut every other year hedges, don't come into that category. The fledglings in that sort of hedge are caught and despatched in very quick order. Which all seems a great shame and leaves me at a loss to understand why I have to treat hedges this way. The two avian success stories here are lapwings and skylarks. I've yet to see either in a hedge.

★★★

Most of my friends who go to the pub and who live in the village,get involved in the local shoot, which is held on Saturdays. Short days and early dark evenings mean that at the end of the shooting day they all get into the pub, 'for one', on their way home. It takes them about three or four hours, this one drink, then they leave cheerily for home. So it is quite common, at this time of year, for the pub to be deserted on Saturdays, later on in the evening. But one of my friends' wives makes it down one Saturday evening. She tells me that she was upstairs getting changed to go to the pub and she heard her husband arrive home. When she went downstairs, her husband was asleep in the chair and various of three wet Labradors were sprawled out on the floor in front of the fire. She kicked his slippered feet, 'Are you taking me to the pub?' He just grunted and settled deeper in the chair. So she tried again and got the same result. She told me what she said next but I won't repeat it. 'Well, I'm going anyway, I'll go and sit by Roger, he'll be there.' (She knew I'd be there and she knows I'm harmless.) I popped her home after and she phoned me next day. 'When I got back in, he was still asleep in exactly the same position. The only bit of his slippers that the dogs hadn't eaten were the two zips. And he hadn't felt a thing.'

CHRISTMAS 2015

Our tree has been up since the first of December. It will be there until the middle of January. That's six or seven weeks that I can't see out of the window. My family reckon that I'm so grumpy at Christmas that I make Victor Meldrew look like a party animal. It always irritates me, and always has, when people who work in other industries ask how long I have off for Christmas. They always seem to have at least a week, a week that doesn't seem to impact on their annual leave and they are always surprised when I say that I will be working every day.

I suppose that that is where my aversion comes from. We've always had someone working for us but we have always made sure that they had Christmas off. In winter there is a full day's work every day on a dairy farm so if Christmas should fall next to a weekend, there's four days without any help. (They would all have helped if we'd asked but we liked them to have Christmas off, it was a sort of thank you.) It's one of the ironies of life on a dairy farm that when something breaks or gets a puncture, it will always happen at a weekend or Christmas when all the people who keep your farm going disappear for a week. The vet doesn't disappear but he's about the only one. It's something you can rely on; if something can go wrong, it will.

I remember one Christmas morning I was putting out the silage for the cows with the loader. At the end of the yard is a small paddock and the bull and a couple of heifers were living out there. I was feeding them silage every day and I had what we call a ring feeder just the other side of the gate. A ring feeder is a sort of circular manger that you put fodder in and cattle put their heads through some bars so that they eat the fodder without wasting any. The bull had his head through the bars and his head would not come back out. I carried on feeding the cows whilst I considered my options. Normally I would have cut out one bar with an electric angle grinder, but the feeder was 50 yards from the nearest power point. Next option was a hacksaw and to cut it off by hand but I could see that when the bull raised his head the feeder came off the ground, so in theory, if he wanted to, he could run off around the paddock with the feeder on his head whilst I sawed away at the bar. I quickly dismissed that option. I decided that if he could get his head through the gap, his head should, in theory, go back out.

I'd finished feeding the cows now so I got the biggest grab full of silage I could get and I took it down to the bull. I put the boom as high as I could get it and I dropped the silage on the bull's head. He was so surprised that he shot backwards and his head was free. I was well pleased with myself, still am. Looking back at the incident and the fact that it still stands out as the highlight of a lifetime of Christmas days is really quite sad.

★★★

It doesn't apply these days as our milk is collected in the early evening, but for years and years we were first pick-up at eight o'clock. To have your milk ready for collection in time you always had to be out of the kitchen door before 5. But on Christmas Day the drivers always asked that they could come an hour early so that their day was finished at a reasonable time. I never had any problem with that (you upset the tanker driver at your peril!), but it did mean that you had to be out on the yard by 4am. I knew of one farmer who refused to do this, he was the only one at a depot with about 20 lorries, so they weren't best pleased with him! It must have cost him dearly because in those days your milk was quantified with a dipstick so it was the driver who decided how much milk you had! But because you started an hour early, you finished your morning's work an hour early as well. I went back into our empty home one morning (the rest of the family were off somewhere distributing glad tidings). There was nothing to interest me on TV, there weren't the choices we have today. 'I know, I'll go to church.' Never again. Not one of them said 'Happy Christmas', but they all said how surprised they were to see me there.

My Christmas days are very different now. It's my son who is working all day. These days, if there is a good film on TV I get to see the end of it, not go out to milk at half way. I've already had my 'big' present. Years ago I told my neighbour's partner that we never have homemade mince pies, that that nice Mr Kipling in the village makes ours. So now she brings me 48 home-made mince pies every Christmas. And I get a kiss. I'm looking forward to watching *The Sound of Music* for the 100th time, I like that nice family to get away safely. Just spare a thought for all those who have to work over Christmas Day, especially the dairy farmers who have to work every other day as well.

I actually quite enjoy Christmas now but I work quite hard not to show it. I've got a grumpy image that I've developed over many years, and I intend to preserve it. So I wish you all a lovely Christmas. But don't tell anyone I did.

2 JANUARY 2016

Stephen, our only full-time employee, has just had two new hips fitted. Two in one go! So, one evening, a Saturday, a couple of days after the operation, I go to see him. He looks quite well, which is good, but he hadn't got any grapes to share, which isn't so good. I ask him how he's feeling, as you do, and he says he's OK until he gets out of bed and tries to walk. He says he goes very light-headed and dizzy and he's afraid that he will fall over. I express surprise that he sees this as a problem. Quite indignantly, he asks why. I remind him that tonight is Saturday evening when he's well used to feeling dizzy and light-headed, and that he often falls over on Saturday evenings and he's not come to any serious harm thus far. Very quickly, he points out, 'But I haven't got the wall around the churchyard to lean on in here.' I go to see him a couple of afternoons a week, but only if there's something good on the telly.

★★★

II was sitting in someone's office the other day when they had another visitor. He was a smartly dressed young man and as soon as he saw me he came across and said 'Hello Roger, nice to see you.' I didn't have a clue who he was. So after he had gone I asked who he was. It was a lad who used to play rugby with us. Little wonder I didn't recognise him, last time I saw him he had a pony tail. It wasn't just any old pony tail, it came down to his waist. It was a pony tail off a very big pony! It got him in a lot of trouble when he played rugby. Opposing players just couldn't resist giving it a bit of a tug.

Turns out that he is now an expert on vintage guns, writes books about them. I saw a vintage gun at work once. We had a clay pigeon shoot once as a fundraiser at the rugby club. I'd not realised that there could be lots of clay pigeon shoots on a Saturday and the people who participate often go to several shoots on the same day. They go from one to the other, participate, then move on to the next, and they are informed later if they have won anything.

Like most pursuits, clay pigeon shooting has its 'uniform'. You have to wear a quilted waistcoat with leather patches at the shoulders, cartridge belts and hearing protection. What particularly struck me was how animated they all were when they lined up to shoot. If animated has a range, they were at the twitchy end.

So the guns all lined up, about eight at a time, and in front of them was a row of bales that protected the person operating the trap, which is what they call the thing that shoots the clay pigeons, and the clays were going away from the shooters, who had to shoot them before they were out of range. (You with me so far?)

What you did, if you were participating was shout 'Pull' when it was your turn, and off the clays would go. So there was lots of nervous energy about as the rapid sequence continued. 'Pull,' bang, bang, 'Pull,' bang, bang and so on.

The next line of shooters took their place and in the middle was a rugby club member who had an old muzzle loader shot gun. So when it came to his turn he shouted 'Pull' and there were two very loud booms, fire belched out of his gun, threatening to set the bales alight and there was such a cloud of smoke that you couldn't see if he had shot anything anyway. You could tell right away that the other shooters didn't like this departure from their norm, they didn't like it at all. But they carried on nevertheless.

Worse was to come: the rapid sequence carried on to the end of the line, then back to the beginning again, back down as far as the man with the muzzle loader. And then it stopped. It stopped because he was still ramming powder, shots and wads down his barrels. Eventually he was ready, shouted 'Pull' and once again his gun belched fire and smoke and roared its approval. It was all too much for some of the other shooters, they stepped out of the line and left to go to the next shoot. I thought it was funny but they took it all very seriously. Possibly too seriously: it's all very well to take your pastimes seriously but not quite so good if you take yourself too seriously as well.

As a dairy farmer, if I took things seriously, I'd never see this next twelve months out! But the farming year now turns once more, and in all truth, I don't think I'll ever tire of it....

Also published by Merlin Unwin Books

A View from the Tractor Roger Evans £12 hb / £6.75 ebook

A Farmer's Lot Roger Evans £12 hb / £6.75 ebook

Over the Farmer's Gate Roger Evans £6.75 ebook

Myddle *The Life and Times of a Shropshire Farmworker's Daughter* Helen Ebrey £12

Much Ado About Mutton Bob Kennard £20 hb

A Most Rare Vision *Shropshire from the Air* Mark Sisson £14.99 hb

Extraordinary Villages Tony Francis £14.99 hb

The Countryman's Bedside Book BB £18.95 hb

A Job for all Seasons *My Small Country Living* Phyllida Barstow £14.99 hb

My Animals and Other Family Phyllida Barstow £16.99 hb

The Byerley Turk *The True Story of the First Thoroughbred* Jeremy James £8.99 pb / £6.75 ebook

Maynard: *The Adventures of a Bacon Curer* Maynard Davies £9.99 hb / £5.99 ebook

Maynard: *The Secrets of a Bacon Curer* Maynard Davies £9.99 hb / £5.99 ebook

Living off the Land Frances Mountford £12.99 hb

Advice from a Gamekeeper *John Cowan £20 hb*

The Way of a Countryman *Ian Niall £16.99 hb*

The BASC Game Shooter's Pocket Guide Michael Brook £7.99 pb

Available from all good bookshops
For more details of these books: www.merlinunwin.co.uk

The dairy farmers' milk jug *(see page 153)*, hand-painted by Priscilla Kennedy, Tower House, Burley, Shropshire.
01584 861692.
£30 each inc. p&p and a donation on each sale to 'Farmers for Action'.